D1426645

30131 05818161 8

LONDON BOROUGH OF BARNET

INTO
IRAQ

INTO
IRAQ

Michael Palin

HUTCHINSON
HEINEMANN

ON THE ROAD AGAIN

THE FIRST BOOK I WAS EVER GIVEN WAS *TALES FROM THE Arabian Nights*. I still have it, inscribed 'To Michael, with love from his Daddy, 5th May 1950'. It's a chunky hardback with an alluring cover, showing a girl reading from an open book to an entranced boy; behind them one of the Forty Thieves, sword in his mouth, peers menacingly out from the top of a tall jar. Below them stretches a wide blue sea beside whose shore rise the domes and minarets of a mosque. The cover illustration, and the stories within, not only captivated and enthralled me, they defined in my seven-year-old mind what foreignness was. It was my first experience of the allure of other places.

The world so seductively and dramatically conjured up by A.E. Jackson's colour plates was an Arab world, a Middle Eastern world, and yet, in all my subsequent travels, it remained a world I knew least – that is, until 2022, when my travel plans took an unexpected turn.

For some time various obstacles had prevented me going anywhere at all, including surgery to repair two leaky valves in my heart, followed by the Covid pandemic and the protracted shutdown of world travel. I sat at home, making only two journeys in eighteen months – one as far as Bradford and the other, much more ambitious, all the way to Scotland. My atlas was gathering dust and I was hanging my boots on an ever-higher peg. I worried that, if this went on much longer, I might lose the will to move.

With Neil Ferguson, who directed my series in North Korea five years ago, I tried to keep the flickering flame of another journey alight. Together we looked hungrily at maps and guidebooks, planning journeys more in hope than expectation. We were particularly taken by the idea of travelling to the Middle East – a part of the world neither of us was that familiar with. We even got as far as drawing up quite a detailed itinerary for a series on Syria. Unfortunately, our plans were stymied at the last minute when the Syrian authorities found that I had given money to the White Helmets. That volunteer organisation's work to bring relief to those in bombed and damaged areas was anathema to the Assad regime, and we were denied permission to film.

But before finally folding away the map and bidding farewell to the Middle East, my eye was caught by one of the countries that bordered Syria. Iraq. A number of evocative names sprang out at me – Babylon, Baghdad, Karbala, Ur of the Chaldees and two rivers whose names recurred repeatedly throughout ancient history, the Tigris and the Euphrates.

The Greeks called the region Mesopotamia – '(The Land) between Rivers'. So fertile was the land fed by these rivers that ten thousand years ago it encouraged hunter-gatherers to abandon their previously

nomadic way of life and become farmers, creating in the process the world's first settlements. By 5000 BCE some of the settlements had become the world's first cities. These grew into empires with resounding names – Sumeria, Babylon, Assyria. Though they rose and fell in war and bloodshed, they achieved previously unheard-of levels of sophistication: the first written documents, the measurement of time in units of sixty, complex and magnificent architecture, and the wheel, all had their origins in Mesopotamia.

Yet in recent years these lands had witnessed chaos and dysfunction: the brutal dictatorship of Saddam Hussein, invasion by US- and UK-led forces, internecine conflict between the country's different religious and ethnic groups, and the rise and fall of Islamic State. Iraq was written off by the world's media, and demonised by George W. Bush as one of the three countries on his 'axis of evil'. The cradle of civilisation had become the heart of darkness.

Perhaps this grim tide of events should have dissuaded me from wanting to go. In fact, it made me all the more determined. I wanted to understand how the birthplace of civilisation should have become so riven by conflict. I realised I was as fascinated by the region's present as I was by its extraordinary past. I decided that Iraq should be the focus of my next expedition.

Neil and I agreed that our route through Iraq should follow the river Tigris – one of the country's ancient and modern lifelines – from source to sea: from the mountains of southern Turkey to the shores of the Persian Gulf.

Then, only weeks before we were due to leave, and just as the channels of world travel began to flow again, news came through of Russian tanks rolling into Ukraine. The grip of the pandemic had loosened, only to be replaced by the possibility of a world war.

We briefly wondered whether we should postpone our trip. But the thought that Iraq, too, was a place of conflict whose story could so easily be lost amid competing headlines persuaded us to stick with our plan. Almost exactly two years from the day Boris Johnson announced the first lockdown, I was piling my bags into a car, waving farewell to my infinitely tolerant wife and, once again, heading for Heathrow.

What follows is a day-by-day account of our journey into Iraq, kept in a notebook and on a voice recorder. I owe a great debt of thanks to Mimi Robinson for transcribing my often garbled entries, to Peter Griffin for keeping me safe and healthy, and James Willcox of Untamed Borders for his Iraqi expertise. And most of all to Neil Ferguson for planning, directing and inspiring the film, and my wonderful crew, Jaimie Gramston, Ben Crossley and Doug Dreger, not forgetting Will Smith at ITN and Guy Davies at Channel 5 for their unwavering support and encouragement, and Nigel Wilcockson my tolerant, patient publisher, who saw this book through.

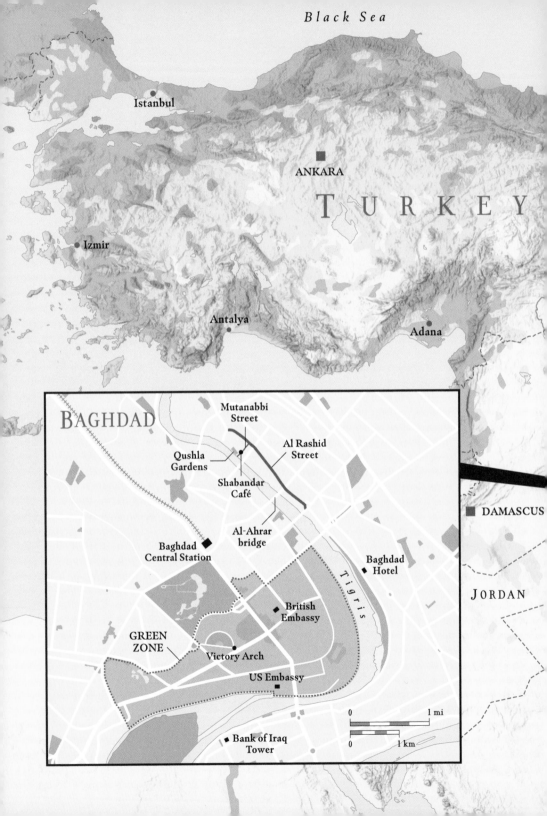

GEORGIA

ARMENIA AZERBAIJAN

■ TBILISI

■ YEREVAN
YEREVAN

■ BAKU

*Caspian
Sea*

Euphrates

Elâziğ
Lake Hazar

Sivrice
Diyarbakir
Tigris
Hasankeyf

Ömerli
Mardin Midyat
Silopi

Duhok

Akre
Darashakran
Refugee Camp

Mosul
Erbil

Baba Gurgur

*Makhoul
mountains*
Kirkuk

Tigris

SYRIA

Euphrates

IRAN

Tikrit

Samarra

Duluiyah

■ BAGHDAD

I R A Q

Karbala Babylon
Tigris

Najaf

Nasiriyah
Al-Qurnah

Euphrates

Ur

SAUDI ARABIA

*Former extent of
marshlands occupied
by the Marsh Arabs*

Basra
Al Faw

KUWAIT

*Persian
Gulf*

KUWAIT
CITY

0   50   100   150 mi

0   100   200 km

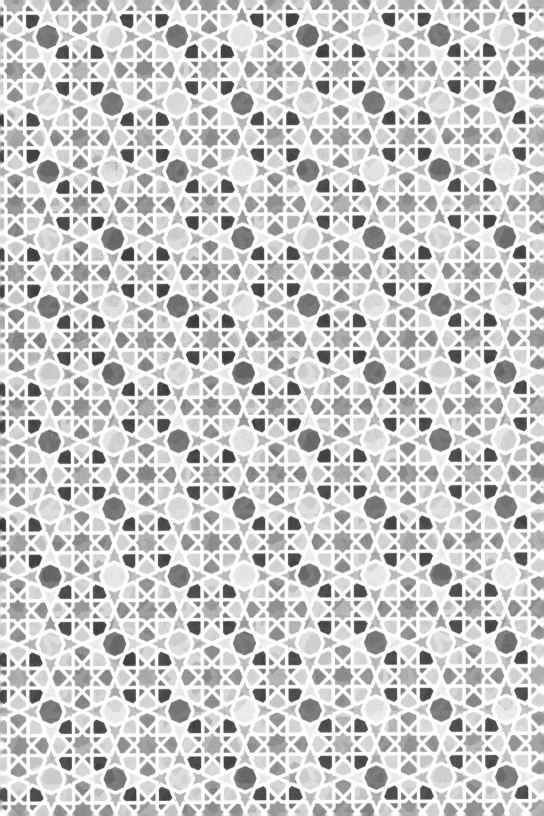

DAY 1

الْيَوْمُ الأَوَّلُ

Monday 14th March

I'M IN ISTANBUL. IT'S A BITTERLY COLD MORNING.
Something I hadn't expected on a trip to Iraq. Our hotel is small, neat
and feels more like a ski lodge. Snow has been partly cleared from the
driveway, leaving deadly patches of slipperiness.

It's still dark.

No time for breakfast. Straight to the airport. Opened less than
four years ago, it covers a vast area of what was once state-owned
forest. Everything about it is big and swanky. The control tower is over
three hundred feet high and in the shape of a tulip, Turkey's national
flower. The place is packed.

We're on an internal flight, which ought to make life straight-forward, but we swiftly discover that every piece of our filming equipment – which was laboriously scrutinised yesterday when we arrived from London – has to be laboriously scrutinised again. The combination of background noise, breath-stifling protective mask and lack of breakfast hits me suddenly and after I get to my feet I find myself so unsteady that I have to pause and reach for support.

My state of health and physical preparedness for the journey have been on my mind for some time. I've done all I can to keep fit, but there's been no way of knowing how I'll shape up until we're on the road. A wobble on Day One isn't a good start.

I put my little turn down to dehydration, and, sure enough, after

water, coffee and juice on the ninety-minute flight to Elâzığ in central Turkey, I feel re-energised.

Istanbul is the only place on this journey that I've been to before. From now on, until we reach Basra, everywhere I visit will be for the first time.

Elâzığ is set amongst snow-covered highlands. It's over three thousand feet above sea level and is home to two hundred thousand people. As we drive to our hotel I hear the sound of a muezzin's call to prayer. I am reminded that despite modern Turkey being founded on non-sectarian lines, 90 per cent of her people are Muslim. I am also reminded that the current president, Recep Tayyip Erdoğan, has done much to bring religion back into Turkish politics.

We drive out to the starting point of our story, the lake from which the river Tigris begins its journey to the Gulf. Grey cloud drifts low over snow-white mountainsides and frequent wintry showers blot out the landscape altogether.

We could be in Iceland.

Then, as we start filming, a transformation. The low cloud lifts and all at once Lake Hazar is revealed in all its grandeur. Its waters turn silvery in the sun, as befits the source of one of the world's great rivers. Remote and quietly spectacular.

Funda, our Turkish fixer, tells me that Hazar is the only natural lake in a land of reservoirs. Which straight away raises one of the issues we shall be dealing with throughout our journey. The water that gathers in these Turkish uplands is a vital and most valuable resource, not just for Turkey, but for its neighbour as well. Indeed, it is as essential to the life of Iraq now as it was ten thousand years ago. How it is husbanded is therefore of enormous significance to both countries.

I record my first piece to camera with the dark waters of the lake stretching behind me. I struggle to encapsulate all that is so important about this place, and why we are here. I'm aware that I haven't done this sort of thing for a while and I'm a little rusty.

Back at the hotel in Elâziğ we all get together for dinner. Everyone is glad that we are finally off. To bed early, hoping to catch up on lost sleep. However, the prospect of a pre-dawn start tomorrow and an alarm clock that is falling apart keeps me awake.

DAY 2 اليوم الثاني

Tuesday 15th March

WE'RE PACKED UP AND ON THE ROAD AT A QUARTER TO SIX.
It's still bitterly cold, but we have a railway journey to look forward to, which always raises my spirits. At a little station called Sivrice we pick up the overnight sleeper from Ankara which will take us east and south and a few miles closer to the Iraqi border. I walk through the train to the grandly named dining car, which turns out to be more of a grandly named café. On the way I pass still-slumbering passengers, draped across their seats, legs extended out into the aisle. At one double seat

a young couple lie coiled together, fast asleep. As the light comes up, a group of women bring their elaborate breakfast into the café car and seeing our eyes widen at such a spread ask us if we'd like to share. It's certainly far beyond anything the train can provide and we tuck in to home-made cakes and pastries, salads and dips, washed down with sweet tea. There's an air of celebration about the ladies. They're all of middle age, on their way from Ankara to see the south-eastern cities of Turkey. Husbands left behind, hence much laughter.

I'm finding Turkish pronunciation tricky. Consonants seem to be swallowed. So, Elâziğ, which we've just left, sounds like Ellzu, and Diyarbakir, where we are to spend the night, is more like Jarbaku.

The train runs through a succession of gorges in the red granite rocks, disappearing every now and then into a network of short tunnels.

When we emerge from these canyons we are out on the flat, between hedgeless green fields that stretch away on either side.

Diyarbakir station is quite impressive, built by Turkish Railways in the 1930s in art-deco style. There are comfortable chairs in a waiting area by the entrance, but no one is using them save for a marmalade cat with a black patch on his nose, who apparently waits for every train, always in the same chair.

Diyarbakir, a city I confess I'd never previously heard of, is the capital of Kurdish Turkey and is a place of character and characters. It is part-ringed by a magnificent city wall almost five miles long, with barbican towers and square keeps, still looking impressive after a thousand years. Below the walls is a handsome ten-arched stone bridge from which we see the Tigris in motion for the first time. It's wide and healthy and looks already like a river of substance as it races beneath the bridge and away towards Iraq. On its banks are terraces lined with tables and chairs. This must be a fine place to sit out in summer, but today it feels bleak. The chill of a north wind is keeping all but a few hardy souls away.

We walk into the bazaar area and find ourselves beneath a corrugated plastic roof in an enclosure entirely devoted to cheese. It's much of a muchness in terms of colour and texture: various shades of white, from cream to pale yellow, laid out in prodigious stacks and odd shapes. Some cheeses look like white sausages. Others are coiled or plaited like rope. One of the cheese sellers is easily roused into a passionate rant about the deficiencies of his country's president. He blames Erdoğan for all ills, especially those of the cheese industry.

As we walk outside there is Mr Erdoğan's likeness, secured to a lamp post. He looks into the middle distance with bland authority, smart in his crisp white shirt and red tie. I ask Funda about his popularity. It sounds rather like Brexit: 49 per cent really hate him, she says, and 51 per cent really like him.

We wander amongst shops, which at this end of the main street are small and intimate. Bulging sacks of walnuts, pomegranates, olives, dried apricots, melons and aubergines stand outside.

Further on the street becomes flashier, the shops become stores and an air of comfortable prosperity takes over. It's very much a modern city, though a few of the old Ottoman buildings still stand. We have lunch in what was a graceful and elegant stone hammam, a bathhouse. Now tables are set out beneath its tall, domed roof, and lunch is served by waiters in uniform.

As we leave a gaggle of young boys accosts us. They wave packets of tissues at us and shout, 'You have money? You have money?' until one of the waiters comes out and clears them away.

'They always here,' he says, shaking his head apologetically.

Not far away is the cultural and religious heart of the city centred around the impressive mosque, Ulu Cami. It was built by the Seljuk

Turks in the eleventh century. Sculptures of lions and bulls decorate the entrance and steps lead down into a courtyard, which despite an eclectic mix of architectural styles, including Roman and Byzantine columns and tall-windowed libraries at either end, has a soothing and harmonious calm. As worshippers wash their feet before prayer, children race in and out of the arcades, and parents stop to gossip. There's a busy unselfconsciousness about religion here.

We go on to somewhere much less restful, but no less full of busy unselfconsciousness: a Mangal bar. Here I meet a young woman called Dilan and we sit and chat as the food we order is cooked on a charcoal fire inches away from us.

The bar seems to be entirely run by young men, probably all from the same family, busily rushing through a stream of punters, mainly lone males ranging from businessmen to labourers and one very old, very distinguished man who, unlike everyone else, seems in no hurry at all.

I take Dilan's advice and, along with the obligatory salads and dips, choose a liver kebab. It's delicious.

Dilan is a Kurdish nationalist, bitterly critical of the government's policy of assimilation. Erdoğan wants everyone in Turkey to be Turkish, but 60 per cent of the people in this town are Kurds, not Turks. The Kurds have their own language, their own traditions, and their own long history that straddles the borders of several modern-day countries, from Turkey to Iraq and from Iran to Syria. Dilan dreams of independence, but would settle for greater autonomy, a relationship with Turkey similar to that between England and Scotland.

As we leave, some of the young men crowd around. They have translation apps on their phones.

'Where you from?'

London.

'London is beautiful.'

I nod appreciatively.

'You are beautiful. How old you are?'

When I tell them I'm seventy-eight, they gaze hard at their phones as though what I've told them is mathematically impossible.

Back at the hotel we have PCR tests, obligatory for entering and leaving Iraq. We've mixed with a lot of people these past few days, and should any of our socialising make for a positive result our journey could still be scuppered. For now, the more urgent problem is the extraordinary ferocity of the test. Instead of smoothing the inside of the nostril, our nurse stabs the applicator in there. The foyer of the hotel rings with the sharp cries of grown men holding their noses.

DAY 3

اليوم الثالث

Wednesday 16ᵗʰ March

TODAY WE ARE OFF TO SEE ONE OF THE MAN-MADE changes that has so affected the Tigris in recent years, and that has had such enormous consequences for the supply of water to Turkey and its neighbour. What they call the South-Eastern Anatolia Project began thirty years ago and there are now twenty-two dams at various points along the course of the Tigris, the intention being to boost agriculture in the region, and also to harness the river's might to generate electricity.

My *Rough Guide to Turkey*, now some fifteen years old, points us towards 'the spectacular ruined settlement of Hasankeyf' which 'contains remarkable mediaeval remains of Seljuk, Arabic and Kurdish origin' but warns of it being threatened by the proposed construction of the Ilisu dam. 'Fortunately,' it concludes, 'the international outcry, plus the parlous state of Turkey's finances, reprieved the site for the time being.'

Since then they have found the money from somewhere and with a marked lack of international outcry, Hasankeyf has disappeared beneath the water. After a long drive across the featureless Tigris flood-plain we arrive in 'new' Hasankeyf. In an empty street of recently built houses we meet a nineteen-year-old man called Sali. He is slim and has a dark, intense gaze. He invites us into the house to which he and his family were moved when their village was engulfed. His anger is palpable. His father, who was in his seventies, died soon after they were moved. Negotiations are still ongoing for compensation money, which so far has been paltry, as they had rented, rather than owned, their house.

Nothing he says can quite match the eloquence of the photo which covers one wall of the house. It shows a colourful neighbourhood climbing up a slope by the river. There is a bridge to one side and bougainvillaea trails along the walls. The narrow streets are eye-catchingly attractive, with a distinct Mediterranean flavour.

That's where he used to live before the waters rose. Now he is unemployed.

I am taken out on to the waters beneath which Sali's home town and some two hundred smaller villages now lie. Around us is an arid basin of bare brown slopes. You can still see tarmacked roads running into the water.

Hasankeyf used to be a tourist attraction, and on the other side of town from Sali's house they are spending a lot of money constructing replicas of the drowned old town's buildings, which people once came a long way to see. Trees have been planted and roads are being paved. Nothing, however, can disguise the fact that the real thing has gone for ever.

Or maybe not. The irony is that since the Ilisu dam was built, water levels have been falling rather than rising. They're now two hundred feet lower than when the project was completed. If this trend persists, maybe the minarets and bridges of old Hasankeyf will emerge, like a ghost, from the trapped waters of the Tigris.

We now turn south again, close to Syria and only a night's stay away from Iraq. This is border country, and as we wend our way through

busy towns like Midyat and Ömerli there's a very visible security presence. Police checkpoints, army barracks and government buildings are
girdled by twelve-foot-high blast-proof concrete slabs. These towns
were the heartlands of Kurdish resistance to Turkey. Since the 1980s
a violent insurgency led by the Marxist PKK, or Kurdistan Workers'
Party, a militant nationalist group deemed terrorists by the government
in Ankara, has cost some fifty thousand lives. Now the security imper-
ative is more geared to any activity by the militant Islamist members of
ISIS (also known as ISIL, Islamic State and Daesh) spilling across the
border from northern Syria and Iraq. The sight of sandbagged buildings
and police with weapons drawn reminds me, unhappily, of Northern
Ireland in the 1980s.

Home for our fourth night is Mardin, a dramatically situated hill-
town looking out over the great floodplain of the Tigris and Euphrates.
It is the gateway to Mesopotamia.

We're staying at a historic hotel called the Mardius. It's high up on the hill and our director is anxious to film me looking out over Mesopotamia at sunset. Unfortunately, because of the precipitous nature of the town, it's impossible to drive our vehicles up to the main doors of the hotel. So a mad sprint ensues, from the main road up picturesquely winding alleys, with lethally icy steps, racing past bemused donkeys and charging into the hotel like Viking raiders. Yet more steps and at last the balcony and the sunset, and the view.

When we've had time to breathe we are able to take in a beautiful old palace, built on several levels, with walls of warm brown sandstone and stone arches and balustrades. Until recently it belonged to a family of whom only one aged lady remained. The man whose dream it was to open it as a hotel finally persuaded her to sell. She did so on one condition: that alcohol should never be served on the premises. So we opt to eat, and drink, at a noisy restaurant in the town. Our director

dins into us that this is a treat, a final treat before the rigours of Iraq. Our PCR tests, obtained at such nasal cost, have all come back negative. We're good to go to Iraq tomorrow.

My room is fit for a sultan and includes a free-standing bathtub in a vaulted stone bathroom. As I soak luxuriously I realise that, whatever the uncertainties, dangers or lack of comforts that lie ahead, the real excitement of this journey is about to start. Turkey has been kind to us, comfortable and often spectacular. Iraq will be no such soft option. It's a country few people would choose to visit. For me that's one of the best reasons to go there.

My grandson Archie will be sixteen tomorrow. I call him and say I'm sorry I'll miss his birthday, but I'm going into Iraq. He takes it philosophically. 'Don't worry, Grandpa – just stay alive till the next one.'

DAY **4** اليوم الرابع

Thursday 17ᵗʰ March

WE SPEND THE MORNING IN MARDIN. THE TOWN
confidently shows itself off. In the main square a big screen flashes
tantalising images of the delights to be experienced here. Below it a
statue of Kemal Atatürk, the founder of modern Turkey, stands on a
plinth; at its foot a sleeping dog lies flat out. In the market nearby they sell
almonds coloured blue, every kind of fruit, and sausages as big as horse
collars. At the end of an alleyway is a shop full of small birds in cages.

The owner's speciality is pigeons trained to do somersaults in the air, which is quite a bizarre sight. It's not an easy way to make a living, he explains, as very often the pigeons not only won't somersault, but fly off, never to be seen again. The best performers, he tells us, are the dark ones with brown breasts. He calls them 'Mosul pigeons'.

Tomorrow, inshallah, we shall actually be in Mosul.

The Iraqi border is about two and a half hours away by car from smart, urbane Mardin. It's a dull drive to start with, through flat fields of young green wheat watered by the Tigris. Then we're into low hills, with mountains beyond. The road winds through the grubby city of Silopi and we find ourselves sharing it with an increasing number of big,

dirty trucks. Iraq is virtually landlocked and railways seem non-existent, so goods have to come in and out by road. In the midst of all this movement we find ourselves criss-crossing the Tigris. Even our heroic river seems a little run-down here, sprawling around marshy islands on which sheep are grazing. A high security fence runs along the riverbank, for at this point the Tigris is the border and the far bank is Syria.

By mid-afternoon we are at the frontier with Iraq. Here an elaborate ritual begins. We have to unload all our bags and equipment and put them into transit vehicles which will take us up to the Turkish border, which we will then cross before transferring everything into a fresh set of vehicles which will take us into Iraq, where we shall reload one last time into the cars that will be carrying us to our hotel.

The whole process takes about four hours before we finally pass through. Bits of paper are waved about, passports checked again and again and the bags examined and re-examined. At points we come close to desperation, feeling doomed to spend the rest of our lives in this vacuum of honking trucks and inexplicable queues and stony-faced officials sitting behind dirty screens.

So when we finally pass beneath a garish pantiled arch and glimpse our Iraqi fixers waiting for us beneath a tall flagpole flying the flag of Kurdistan, there is understandable, if exhausted, jubilation. And when I find that Salar Sabir, our fixer, spent several years in my home town of Sheffield, I feel idiotically pleased to be in Iraq at last.

DAY 5

اليوم الخامس

Friday 18ᵗʰ March

A BRIGHT MORNING. WE'RE GATHERED OUTSIDE THE Rixos hotel in the town of Duhok. 'Candle in the Wind' was playing in the lifts as I checked in last night, and 'Hey Jude' as I rode down to breakfast. Shielded from the road by blast barriers, we're being briefed by James Willcox, whose company, Untamed Borders, specialises in taking people to places most other people don't want to go to. Standing beside him is Peter, ex-army, accompanying us as security and medical escort. No one has suggested that he's here because I'm so old, but I can't help sensing that he's keeping an eye on me. I, in turn, am determined to pretend I'm twenty-eight, not seventy-eight.

James is concerned about our safety in Iraq, as was the hotel's armed security officer who ran a detector under our car before lowering the protective steel plates on the approach road as we arrived last night. James cautions us against loose talk. Never tell anyone we meet which hotel we're staying at or what we're here for. If we want to go

out at night 'don't go without one of us'. My heart sinks a little at this. For me, solitary exploration is one of the greatest pleasures of travel. There will be many checkpoints along the way, we are warned. 'Don't get stressed,' says James, before adding, 'Don't start taking photos, don't get on the walkie-talkies and have some fun, anything like that.'

It's all quite sobering – a reminder that we will be entering areas whose names evoke the worst of human behaviour. The country's second city, Mosul, for example, has been at the centre of violent change for most of this century, enduring civil war, al-Qaeda occupation and, most recently, the brutally severe regime of ISIS/Daesh. They first made their presence felt in Iraq in the aftermath of the US-led 2003 invasion and went on to declare themselves a worldwide caliphate in 2014, seizing large areas of the country in the process. They ran Mosul for three years, before being ejected by government forces with huge loss of civilian lives.

Mosul is where we're going today.

Like many of the vehicles here our lead car has the bulky swollen undercarriage that shows it's been armour-plated. The one I'm in hasn't. They call it a 'softskin'. Nobody seems worried.

Up until now we've been in an area run by the KRG, the Kurdish Regional Government. Now we're moving into territory under the authority of the federal government. This, I'm led to believe, is not a good thing.

By half-past nine we are at our third and most heavily guarded checkpoint. Our papers are examined by a soldier in full body armour, night-vision goggles, Kevlar helmet and with an AK-47 across his chest. He's unimpressed by our credentials and beckons us to pull over and wait in a side channel. Salar gets out and collects our passports for the third time today. I like Salar. Not just because he's lived in Sheffield, but for his temperament, his ability to take all this on without screaming and shouting. Short, compact, with broad, slightly hunched shoulders, he holds himself defensively, his eyes lowered but always darting about, full of wary humour.

The key to these endless security checks is endless patience. No point raising your voice or pointing out that we have a letter of authority signed by the president. The men in charge of the checkpoints have to feel that they rule the world, and that involves taking their time.

The roadside is strewn with rubbish: plastic bags blow backwards and forwards through the fields, like a flock of lost birds. The Tigris runs in parallel with us, but for a while is transformed from a river to a two-mile lake, the Mosul dam, the biggest in Iraq.

On the outskirts of Mosul sheep are grazing on the verges, picking their way around burnt-out cars. On the opposite carriageway a half-mile-long line of cars waits for petrol.

The first sign of the scale of the damage done to this ancient city is the wrecked shell of a huge hospital. It's shocking and unmissable. Because of its size and prominent position by one of the Tigris bridges, it was used as a base by Islamic State snipers, and was the last building to fall in the battle to free the city. Medical staff and patients were used as human shields and many lost their lives as the Iraqi army, backed by US- and UK-led coalition firepower, flushed out the insurgents. All this barely five years ago.

Around the skeleton of the hospital, debris has been bulldozed into long piles. Sparrows perch on stacks of twisted barbed wire as if they were on a country hedge.

We're taken to the old city where, by the banks of the Tigris, whole neighbourhoods were destroyed in hand-to-hand fighting. What remains

amongst the ruins are heaps of rubble mixed in with clothes, comics, furniture, school books. Some of the narrow streets have been cleared, others remain impassable, blocked by collapsed concrete walls leaning at odd angles. A young girl comes up, curious to see what we're doing here. A boy joins her, eyeing me quizzically. He and his friend have catapults. He lets me have a go, grinning and laughing as I inexpertly send a stone skimming across the road. I walk a little further on, away from the film crew, and come across two children sitting at the doorstep of what is left of a house. The boy is seven or eight, the girl older. Eleven or twelve, I guess. They sit silently together, he with a shy smile, she impassively, showing no emotion. I ask if I can take their picture.

The girl nods, solemnly. It's then, as I frame the two of them, sitting amongst the debris of a roofless house, the wall behind them studded with bullet holes, that I find myself unable to contain my own emotion. Tears well up and I have to turn away.

Not that tears are what they want here. Or not from us, anyway. They want to know who we are and where we're from. The solemn girl and the smiling boy are soon joined by others and I feel like a Pied Piper in reverse as my stroll turns into a guided tour. They lead me to a house, one of the few still intact, and beckon me inside. There, in a tall room, shuttered against the sun, I find a circle of older women, sitting on the floor, preparing lunch. Women are so shielded from the public gaze in Iraq that I feel perhaps I shouldn't be here. I bring my right hand up to my heart, bow and make to retreat, but they urge me to join them, smiling broadly, clearly rather excited by my interest. Children cluster around, and there is much banter that I can't quite interpret.

My lack of understanding seems to entertain more than frustrate them. I want to ask them about the barbarity they must have witnessed here and the friends and family they must have lost in these streets, but it seems quite inappropriate. Their mood is upbeat – celebratory, even. They enjoy being taken notice of. They want me to sit and share food with them and I feel bad that our time is so short.

Outside, I have some photos taken with the children. I'm not naive enough to think that all is well in the ruins of Mosul, but the quite spontaneous welcome we've received suggests that there is a resilience here that is stronger than anger.

Our fixer Salar is visibly angry though. People died in awful ways here. Families took shelter in the basements of their houses only to find that when the house above them collapsed they were trapped beneath concrete and rubble. Many starved to death that way. He surveys the still-shattered neighbourhood and complains that UNESCO funds are going to the repair of the mosques and not to the homes of the poorest people, who suffered so much.

I see more of Mosul in the company of a young man called Harith. Early twenties, dressed casually but carefully in navy Oxford shirt, jeans and black leather jacket, he has a neatly trimmed beard and, as with most young Iraqi men, his hair is dark and lustrous and well cut.

His father's a doctor, his mother also works in the health sector. He talks eloquently of the three years of ISIS occupation. He had to change his Western clothes for a robe, he couldn't listen to music, and though he managed to hold on to his phone, he could have been arrested and tortured had he been discovered using it. His education came to a standstill, something he particularly resented. 'Mosul was a well-educated city.' Worst of all was the random brutality. A physically handicapped friend of his was taken away, imprisoned and killed for no reason. In the centre of town homosexuals were tossed from the roofs of buildings whilst a crowd was forced to watch. He aged twenty years in those three years, he tells me.

All this from a young man whose favourite English author is Jane Austen.

Now some things are better, and there is a determination to rebuild. But it's proceeding very slowly. The university library has just reopened, but of the five bridges across the river only two are usable. Harith wants to get out, to go, ideally, to the UK to study English. It's sad to hear this in a way, because Harith is just the sort of bright, educated young man Iraq needs if it's to rebuild.

We leave the wrecked old city, and he takes me to a riverside café called Mosul Forest Gardens. I can't see a forest and the gardens stand dry around fountains that no longer fount, but the covered terraces leading down to the river are full of family groups eating and drinking. Some of them are out on the Tigris in sedate double-decker boats. For the more intrepid there is the shrieking thrill of being flung around in power boats.

Harith introduces me to his friend Adel. 'Like the singer but without the "e",' says Adel, smiling broadly. Both are very much into rock music and English novels. They express deep dislike for their politicians. Neither of them smokes or drinks alcohol and neither has a girlfriend. Young men, they tell me, cannot be seen alone with a girl unless they are engaged.

I drink a huge glass of fresh orange juice and we keep each other company as the sun begins to go down.

On the way out of Mosul, we see work going on to rebuild the famous, much revered al-Nouri mosque into which UNESCO, as Salar pointed out, is sinking a huge amount of money. Their aim is to create a public complex worthy of the intellectual heritage of this historic city. 'We want to raise the spirits of the people of Mosul,' I was told by the chief of works. As we head out of this brutalised city I can't help wondering if there aren't better ways to raise the spirits of the people, like clearing the rubble their families died in.

We drive past the shell of another vast mosque complex, built by Saddam Hussein and never finished.

DAY **6**

Saturday 19th March

WE REACHED ERBIL, SEAT OF THE GOVERNMENT OF
Kurdistan, late last night. Its gleaming, flashy neon streets seemed to
flaunt a confidence that was in short supply in Mosul, and this morning
the difference is rubbed in as we visit one of the partly completed
gated communities a half-mile or so from our hotel. This one's called
Dream City. *'Where architects make your dreams come true,'* proclaims
the sales board outside. We peer in through locked steel gates at an
only slightly downsized version of the White House. Another edifice
boasts a facade containing everything from neo-classical balustrades to
plate-glass bay windows, enclosed on three sides by a huge concrete
carapace that creates the effect of a half-opened present.

The reason for this brazen opulence is not far away. On an adjoining road stand three ten-storey office blocks with green tinted windows, all belonging to Chevron Oil. And oil is what Iraq is all about. The potential of the Mesopotamian oilfields had been known about since the early years of the last century, and it was the reason why the victorious Allies in the First World War, especially Britain and France, were so keen to step into the power vacuum created by the fall of the Ottoman empire. The French took Lebanon and Syria and the British lumped together the three city states of Mosul, Baghdad and Basra and called it Iraq. Much to the dismay of the Kurds who had held out hopes of independence, their homeland, Kurdistan, was also incorporated.

To keep them from making common cause with neighbouring Kurdish populations, the Iraqi Kurds were given a degree of

self-government denied to their counterparts in Turkey and Iran. That autonomy continues today. So strong is their sense of identity that they have their own flag: a shining sun superimposed on red, white and green stripes.

The biggest of all flies from a 60-foot flagpole in the Citadel at the heart of the city. It stands on a massive high-walled mound which has risen, one settlement upon another, since the first known occupation of Erbil eight thousand years ago. Salar used to live here with his family. He's a Turkmen, or ethnic Turk – one of a three-million minority in Iraq who emigrated here from central Asia. The Citadel has always been a cosmopolitan place, with Turkmen, Arabs and Jews living side by side. Currently it's being restored and there's just one family left behind the mighty walls. According to Salar they're only

there because the city authorities had promised not to evacuate the whole populace during the works. The token family are reported to be very unhappy.

Tomorrow is the spring equinox, and the start of the Kurdish New Year. Government offices are closed and, as the celebrations get under way, crowds are starting to gather. We join the throng down below the Citadel in the Qaysari Bazaar. Labyrinthine passageways are filled with stalls and shops. I'm not allowed to pass the Kurdish costume seller without trying on one of the silver, grey and black

keffiyehs, or headscarves, that the men wear with their national dress. Nor can I visit the bazaar without stopping for a glass of tea at the atmospheric old tea-room, whose walls are filled with photos of those who have drunk here over the years. Sitting by the doorway, in his usual place, is a regular, a man in late middle age, who, like Salar, has spent some time in the UK. I ask him where and he replies, with some affection, 'Margate.'

'Margate?'

'Yes, Margate.' He elaborates: 'And the Kent area.' He points out an

even older man, who sits opposite. 'That man has been to Maidstone! He knows Maidstone!'

I feel as though I'm in a Python sketch.

Outside, on Shar Garden Square, with its arcades and fountains and clocktower modelled on Big Ben, is a café packed to the rafters. Down below, the punters are all men, drinking tea and sucking on nargilehs, or hookahs. En masse they seem a little intimidating, and I feel more at ease on the first-floor balcony, where men, women and children mix. I take tea with Huda Sarhang. She's small, bright,

energetic. Unlike Harith and Adel in Mosul she is not completely disillusioned with politics. She can see herself running for election, though she would want to do so as an independent. But, she bemoans, unless you have the right connections it's impossible to get on. For now, she's making a living from producing candles based on the shape of the local tea glasses. They are proving very popular.

I ask her about the apparent segregation of men and women at the café. She says I shouldn't read too much into that. She can sit wherever she wants. She just feels more comfortable up here. She also

points out that the nargilehs that so many men have taken to never used to be a part of Kurdish culture. They've come in from Lebanon, Syria and the Arab countries. Kurdistan, she says, is the best place for Kurds to live. They have more rights here than the Kurds in Turkey or Iran. They can move freely, speak Kurdish and educate their children however they want. Of course, independence is the goal.

'Maybe not in my lifetime,' she smiles, 'but I hope so.'

I feel she'd make a very good ambassador for her people.

One of the shops where she sells her craft candles is a tailor's called Mr Erbil, where by coincidence we've arranged to film later. They're making me a jacket to measurements sent ahead from London. Considering this arm's length tailoring process, they've produced a very good fit. Both proprietors speak excellent English and wear tweed jackets. Their shop would not be out of place in Savile Row or Notting Hill. It's beautifully designed and immaculately kept. Their aim is to build on a Kurdish tradition of fine-cut tailoring and use of good-quality materials. They make a few adjustments and promise to have the finished product ready before we leave Erbil.

As if to underline the city's cosmopolitan buzz there's a sushi night at the hotel tomorrow.

{ اليوم السابع DAY 7 }

Sunday 20th March

THE ONLY PLACE WHERE TRUE KURDS CELEBRATE
Nowruz, the New Year festival, is in the town of Akre, in the mountains seventy miles north of Erbil. Though the most spectacular part
of the ceremony will not take place until dusk, we've been advised to
make our way there early, as the town and its roads will be packed and
parking places non-existent.

In the flatlands, before one of the checkpoints, is a huddle of huts
with blue plastic roof coverings. I ask our driver what this is. Military?
It turns out to be Darashakran, a camp for Syrian refugees, some of the
three million in Iraq displaced by war and conflict. There are almost a
thousand people in this camp alone, with no heat and little food. How
long will they be here, in the middle of nowhere? My driver shrugs and
shakes his head.

The range of fractured, boulder-strewn mountains which tower over Akre spring quite suddenly from the plains below. Once you are amongst them you sense how important they are to the town and what a spectacular natural theatre they provide for the Nowruz celebrations. Already a column of people is winding its way up to one of the summits, from which they have unfurled a sixty-foot long Kurdish flag which spills down over the rocks.

On a lower hill opposite, the media are gathering. This is the biggest public event of the Kurdish year and mike-clutching reporters are already at work setting the scene. Sharing the same hilltop are the creators of what I've been told will be the biggest firework display in the history of Nowruz.

As the day progresses, fever mounts. More and more cars arrive. When the town streets are full, newcomers park precariously up the various mountain roads. In the main square increasingly harassed police, in tight navy-blue uniforms, are trying to keep the way clear for arriving VIPs. Children are haggling with dodgy-looking men selling firecrackers. Women are parading in full, sparkling brocaded dresses, coatless despite the cold. An old lady carrying her shopping up the hill pauses to watch an army SWAT security team being briefed.

The main celebrations are due to take place at dusk and climax with a firework display and procession with flaming torches up to the top of the mountain, but there are plenty of people jumping the gun. Firecrackers are going off all over the place; thunderous explosions shake the streets, and more and more people are clambering up the paths to join the crowds jostling for a place at the top of the

mountain. Another huge flag has been unfurled and beside it the word 'PESHMERGA' is picked out in huge letters. Meaning 'those who face death', it was originally coined by those fighting for an independent Kurdistan. Now they're the official Kurdish military forces.

It's impossible not to be carried along by the fervour, and as the afternoon draws on we start to squeeze our way through the crowds in the square and up to a good vantage point on the mountainside. On the way we pass people watching from balconies that the locals have generously opened up for the day. We end up amongst an expectant crowd squashed into an area of hillside very close to the area where the torches will be lit and handed out. These torches, long poles each with a bundle of petrol-sodden rags tied at the top, stand against a rock. As the time for the procession nears there are increasingly loud and

acrimonious arguments about who is eligible to carry them. Would-be bearers have to have applied for the role and been given a ticket, but this bureaucratic process falls by the wayside as the hysteria mounts. Jaimie, camera on shoulder like Long John Silver's parrot, stands heroically in the midst of all this, waiting for what looks increasingly like impending mayhem.

And mayhem it proves to be. As the sun sinks the signal is given, torches are seized with furious enthusiasm and carried en masse to a fire to be lit. This takes place in a confined space on a slippery mountainside with noise all around. Deafening shouts, explosions, even the sound of tracer fire from somewhere (apparently a number of people were determined to shoot down the TV companies' drones – including ours).

As people stumble past I'm aware of a torch brushing close enough to singe my hair, as well as a man in Kurdish dress perilously balanced on a rock, holding two blazing torches and waving a flag. A cry of alarm goes up as a boulder dislodged by those higher up the mountain comes tumbling down, just missing a group of us. Music blares out, searchlights stab the sky, and everyone gets in everyone else's way. But somehow the procession materialises, and its zigzag progress as it snakes its way up to the summit is wonderful to watch.

Then the fireworks begin and sound and colour echo and flash all around. One can only hang on for dear life and watch with breathless admiration at what is being wrought here, as the mountains of Akre become a cauldron of noise and light and joyous celebration.

At the end of it all, as we walk back into town to pack up our gear, past firemen extinguishing firecracker-ignited piles of rubbish, I ponder that nothing like this could pass even the most elementary Health and Safety restrictions back home. But then what makes it a whole lot safer than any similar event in the UK is that no one here is drinking alcohol.

DAY 9 | اليوم التاسع

Tuesday 22nd | March

AFTER A DAY OFF IN THE COMFORTS OF THE TURKISH-owned Divan hotel, Erbil, we leave today for the second, potentially much tougher half of the journey, south to Baghdad, Babylon and Basra.

Salar, our excellent Turkmen fixer, returns home, and to help us through the complex security of central southern Iraq his place is taken by Ammar. He's in his early forties, trim, neat, a journalist for Agence France-Presse and, so we're told, well connected with the country's movers and shakers. He's in at the deep end, for today we head to Kirkuk which my guidebook calls 'the most dangerous city in Iraq'.

First, though, the happy task of collecting my finished jacket from Mr Erbil. One of their tailors has worked on it over the Nowruz holiday and there is relief all round as I stand in front of the mirror. Spot on.

Leaving behind the seductive comforts of Erbil we hit the road for Kirkuk. We're once again in Iraqi government territory and the soldiers and police manning the checkpoints are backed up by armoured cars.

Courtesy of Ammar's contacts at the very top of government we have a letter of authorisation to pass through the country, but this doesn't seem to have much of an effect on the helmeted, masked faces that peer suspiciously into our cars before indicating that we must pull over. Then a game begins, which involves the handing over of our passports, deliberately intense scrutiny of our authorisation letter, unnecessarily long phone calls to confirm it whilst we are kept parked up amongst piles of rubbish, as an endless succession of trucks rumbles past.

The countryside we're travelling through grows more menacing as we head south. Walled and sandbagged bases, trench networks, lookout towers and armoured vehicles with machine guns poking out all point to fear of a threat that has not gone away.

We are today going to the heart of what created Iraq and what keeps her going. Oil. Kirkuk may look a bit of a mess now, but it has, like so many of the ancient cities of Mesopotamia, an impeccable pedigree. Dating back six thousand years it has been part of many ancient empires – Sumerian, Assyrian, Babylonian and Median. Muslims, Christians and Jews have lived here. The prophet Daniel is buried here. But none of this is as relevant to modern Iraq as what was discovered beneath this particular stretch of desert on 14th October 1927. After years of searching, the Turkish Petroleum Company, a mix of British, French and American interests, struck lucky when a gusher burst out of the ground outside Kirkuk. It took ten days to cap it, by which time 95,000 barrels a day had been spilt across the arid desert.

Nearly a hundred years later, the oil still gushes out of the ground, not just in Kirkuk, but right across the country, making Iraq the fifth-largest producer of oil in the world, after the USA, Russia, Saudi Arabia and Canada.

So what makes it feel like a lower-league player?

Some of the answers are all too obvious as we pay a call to the headquarters of the North Oil Company, one of the bodies made responsible for the production of oil in Iraq, after Saddam Hussein nationalised the industry in 1972.

The company sprawls across a vast area and we chase up various blind alleys before we get to the centre of the operation. It's housed in colonial-style buildings put up by the British almost eight decades ago. They are long and low with wide roofs, and painted in a light brown wash. They remind me of the old Ealing Studios. Same period, I suppose. Nothing much seems to have been done to keep them in good repair.

Our pre-arranged meetings take place in shabby rooms and seem to demand little more than sitting on sofas and drinking tea whilst the man behind the desk demonstrates his importance by pretending he's very busy. Any suggestion of forward movement is invariably problematical. One man alone cannot make a decision. He will be joined by a half-dozen others who stand around and look equally indecisive. It's hard to get a straight answer to even the simplest question. When I ask the head of Public Relations if he can tell me the story of how oil was first discovered, he looks troubled.

'You can find that anywhere.'

But they eventually get their act together and a convoy of cars takes us out on a rare and privileged visit to something few outside the company are allowed to see. It's a saucer-shaped declivity called Baba Gurgur. Ninety metres in circumference, it would be wholly unremarkable were it not for flickering patches of flame at its centre. Naphtha and natural gas deposits have been keeping these fires burning for four thousand years. Herodotus mentions the place in his *Histories*, written in the fifth century BCE. This is where oil was first discovered in 1927. A forest of derricks and flare stacks a mile to the west show that Baba Gurgur is still giving.

Considering that it was, until 1948, the largest oilfield in the world, the significance of what began here goes uncelebrated. There is a faded sign reading '*The Eternal Flame*', but that's about all there is by way of acknowledgement that this is the true birthplace of modern Iraq.

Before we leave North Oil we're taken somewhere I'd very much not expected. In a corner of their rambling campus is a leisure complex,

built by the British for their largely European workforce in the 1950s. It's easy to forget that for a decade or so after the First World War Iraq was a British mandate. Even after the country was granted independence in 1932, its oilfields would have been a playground for Western managers and their families. Now renamed the Baba Cultural and Social Centre, it exudes the atmosphere of a bygone, Enid Blytonish world. As I look from the terrace outside the domed dance hall to the swimming pool below with its high diving boards, changing rooms, and a garden off to one side with recliners and pavilions, I can imagine

suncream and one-piece swimsuits and panama hats and freckled children chasing each other among the trees.

Today, in early March, we're told the place is not yet open for the summer. The pool is empty, the fences rusty and the changing rooms full of leaves. Broken taps drip and there is, once one's imagination is reined in, a deeply forlorn air about the place. Ammar senses my disappointment.

I'm very aware of Ammar's disapproval of what we've seen here. The money from all the oil that lies out there in the desert goes into the pockets of the politicians, not the people. The corruption, he says, is like a plague.

We stay overnight at the Kirkuk Plaza hotel. It's on the corner of the busy main street. A line of palm trees stretches along the central reservation. Veiled women push by beneath big ads for beauty products, modelled by non-veiled, non-Iraqi women displaying perfect teeth. I'd like to go out and join the throng, get the feel of the street life on this busy Kirkuk evening, but we're warned against it. We would stand out too obviously, we are told. We could become targets.

So I take the lift up to my room and decide to watch the world go by from my balcony. Except that my balcony isn't quite finished and to step out might be more dangerous than risking becoming a target.

Kirkuk is a world away from Erbil. There's no alcohol at dinner. And every now and then there's a blackout. But my bed is comfortable enough and I fall asleep easily.

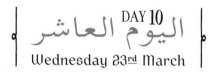

DAY 10
اليوم العاشر
Wednesday 23ʳᵈ March

ALL BEING WELL, WE SHALL BE IN BAGHDAD BY TONIGHT.
And for some romantic reason that thought makes me smile. I think it's
the prospect of seeing for real the city at the heart of so many stories.
On the way, though, we shall be stopping at a place with more sinister
connotations. Tikrit. Another city as ancient as Baghdad but tarred by
its association with Saddam Hussein, who was born there and who,
following the US-led invasion to topple him, was discovered by the
Americans in December 2003 hiding in a hole underground at a village
nine miles away.

There is a slight jumpiness in the air as we load the vehicles
this morning. Our route will take us through the Makhoul mountains,
known to be one of the hideouts of the remaining ISIS/Daesh resistance. Just this week the Iraqi army began an offensive to try and flush
them out. So, we're told, be prepared.

The first problem we encounter is of our own making. Travelling
in convoy is not something our drivers take to. Iraqi men don't like

to follow anyone else. Everyone wants to be the leader. This makes for some early confusion, and more time is spent trying to locate the other vehicles, which all sped off on their own, than actually making progress.

Once we're finally together we encounter the first checkpoint. Hand over passport, wait by the side of the road, no photographs. Then on to a wide, ten-lane highway. However, our hopes that we will now make good progress are abruptly dashed a few miles later when it squeezes down to two. Another checkpoint. Passport. Wait in side lane. No photographs.

Then on through a flat dusty landscape which bears the scars of war. The road surface is scored by deep grooves, which we're told were made by tanks and military vehicles for whom this was a very

active battle area. There are lookout towers and guard posts every other mile. They have a cheap, improvised look to them. Basically made from local materials. Mud, sand and brick hastily piled together and topped with barbed wire to provide some sort of shelter in an exposed and vulnerable terrain. Only the occasional palm tree or flock of dusty brown sheep breaks the monotony. We drive on, darting in and out of a continuous line of huge careering trucks, heading like us for Baghdad. Looking out at the countryside I'm increasingly aware of the sudden change from agricultural land to the desert which comprises more than half the country.

After a while, the Makhoul mountains rise to the east. Less dramatic than I expected, more like low rolling hills. I can see why they might be a hiding place for militias. There is no one else there.

At the fourth checkpoint, with two still to go before Tikrit, something remarkable happens. They're pleased to see us. Ammar always spins some story as he negotiates with the guards at these places. He points me out and I can usually tell by their generally sceptical glances that they don't buy the 'big star visiting Iraq to tell the world what a wonderful place it is' story one bit. This time, however, something has gone very right, and we are not only welcomed with bonhomie, laughter and requests for selfies, we are actually given permission to film the process.

Such cooperation does come at a price. There appear to be some very senior people in the huts by the side of the road this morning. One of them is a general and he wants us all to take tea with him. As we saw yesterday in the offices of North Oil, taking tea is a delaying tactic, much appreciated in the Middle East, but deeply abhorrent to work-obsessed Westerners with a TV series to complete. So we have to

apologise and settle for chummy photos and shoulder clasps with colonels and generals and all those who have made our day at what, to us, will be for even known as Checkpoint Cheerful.

Once we're in Tikrit the smiles fade. We had hoped to be allowed to film some of Saddam's wrecked palaces by the Tigris, but the area is under the control of an Iranian-backed Shia militia who have other ideas. They want us to film the site of what is called the Camp Speicher Massacre, which took place in the city in June 2014 when fighters from ISIL – the Sunni jihadist group Islamic State for Iraq and the Levant – took 1,700 Shia and non-Muslim cadets from the nearby Speicher Camp and murdered all but one of them, throwing many of the bodies into the river. They claimed it was revenge for the death of Saddam Hussein.

The militia have created a display of photos of the victims of this dreadful event. Most of them are faded now, stuck haphazardly to walls

leading down to the Tigris. Young, expectant faces, shot in the back of the head when their lives had barely begun. Telling this story is for me the lowest point of the journey so far. The place, what happened here, the drab commemorative display, the forbidding presence of the unsmiling militiamen preserving their distance but keeping a constant eye on us, all combine to bring home to me the nightmare of Iraq's recent history.

We are still denied permission to film Saddam's palaces. Looking at them through fences and barbed wire one can see interiors blown

apart, but many walls still standing – balustraded, columned, pedimented – breath-taking both for the opulence of their construction and the thoroughness of their shattering.

What on earth are they going to do with these shells of Saddam's vanity? From what I've seen of Iraq so far, I think not a lot.

We leave the city, eating takeaway falafel wraps as we go. No one wants to hang around here.

By mid-afternoon my spirits have risen again as we follow the Tigris to the city of Samarra. Here, at last, is evidence of that continuity of

civilisation which was one of the main reasons I wanted to come to Iraq in the first place. Outside the walls of Samarra's enormous ninth-century mosque, is the Malwiya minaret, over a thousand years old and as beautiful, elegant and distinctive a structure as any I've seen anywhere. The British archaeologist Sir Mortimer Wheeler well described it as 'a great and rather lonely masterpiece'.

The brick-built minaret twirls in a 170-foot spiral to a chamber on top from which the muezzin would once have made his call to prayer.

It's the simplicity and formality and shapeliness of the design which catches the eye, and the fact that after all these years it is still being climbed. I can see a regular line of ant-sized figures ascending and descending, many of them women and children, so I must conquer any vertiginous fears I have and follow them up there.

A little alarmingly, the only rail is against the inside wall. On the outside edge of the steps there is nothing between you and the increasingly widening view. Aesthetically a good call, but when a group of boys chase each other up and down past me I find myself wishing there was something more to hang on to. I must remember I have a camera and a sound recordist following me, so the slightest signs of panic will be mercilessly recorded. The nearer we get to the top, the more attention we are getting from the boys. The usual litany has to be gone through.

'Who are you?'

'What is your name?'

'Where are you from?'

I'm tempted to say I'm not doing interviews, but nothing will assuage their curiosity.

The director would, I know, like me to stand alone and fearless on the totally unprotected flat space at the very top. A thought which terrifies me. But now I'm up here, nearly two hundred feet above the ground, I can't back out. I haul myself up the last few steps and out on to the four-foot-wide, totally unprotected concrete platform, with only the sky above me. At first, my worst fears are confirmed. It is a long way down, and a gusty wind and continued shouts of 'Where are you from?' make my first piece to camera sound like someone admitting to a ghastly crime. But then, quite suddenly, and to my intense relief, I feel secure and can experience the incomparable satisfaction of fear conquered. Not to mention the spectacular view out over the great plain of the Tigris, with the river we've followed for so long winding silvery-white in the late-afternoon sunshine.

If Tikrit was a low point on my journey, the ascent of the minaret at Samarra is, in every sense of the word, a high.

Elation severely tested on the grinding journey to the capital. Our security minders want us there before nightfall, but it's seventy-five miles from Samarra and checkpoints delay us as usual. The pressure tells on all of us. Waiting for the umpteenth time for passports to be returned I notice our driver telling a string of beads and moving his mouth almost imperceptibly. Two heavily armed guards greet each other with a light kiss. No one is in a hurry to clear us through.

The last few miles into the city destroy any romantic notions the name Baghdad might conjure up. Rutted and ripped roadway, no lane markings, cars and trucks swinging all over the place trying to pick out the least bad surface. Complete anarchy, but I see not a single collision.

Finally we turn in to our last checkpoint, at the gate of our hotel. A detection dog sniffs around us, names are checked and the bar slowly raised. High up on the wall ahead of us, picked out in bright red neon, are the best words in the world, *'Baghdad Hotel'*. This long, long day is almost over.

But it still has a few surprises. My room, 332, has someone in it. The staff at reception are apologetic. They meant to give me 323, which they assure me is a suite. Technically, they're right. Aesthetically, it's a horror. A big empty room lit like an interrogation cell with a bedroom attached. I'm too tired to change it now and head downstairs. Arab guests sit together in a brightly lit lounge. Western NGOs, businessmen and tired film crews sit around at low tables near a dimly lit bar, one of the very few places in the Iraqi capital where alcohol is served.

Halfway through our meal there is a fierce crack, like an explosion. Heads flick round. Everyone stops eating. Then there's the sound of hissing and rattling of windows. A storm, I assume, much needed by the look of things. It's still blowing hard when I gratefully lie back in my bed in 323 and sink to sleep.

DAY 11

اليوم الحادي عشر

Thursday 24th March

I WAKE, LIE AND MUSE. I REGRET BEING HARD ON THE hotel last night. I have two rooms and I am in Baghdad, for God's sake. I swing myself out of bed and pull back the curtain, only to reveal what must be the worst view in the world. Pipes, ducts, twisted metal, all covered in dust. The concrete shell of an unfinished block to one side. No glimpse of any living thing.

After breakfast we record a piece to camera in the director's room, which, I find, is not a suite, but a compact and comfortable room with a view looking out over green grass, gardens, trees and the great sweep of the Tigris. Not an air-con vent in sight. Will put in for a transfer from 323 this evening.

Apparently the hour-long storm last night was a sandstorm and not a rainstorm. They've had three already this year, and there is much talk of the way global warming is affecting the country. The desert needs nourishing, not being blown into the city.

Today, by coincidence, we are to visit a family-run farm in Duluiyah, some forty miles north of the capital. A chance to learn more and to see at first hand what Iraq is making of its agricultural potential.

Into the cars, and we scuttle, as best we can, through Baghdad's rush hour and out to the north. We reach the small town of Duluiyah by mid-morning. It's a hot, bright day, and it's a relief after so much time in dusty cities, to find ourselves in rural Iraq, where the streets are quieter and the pace of life distinctly slower. Well-kept gardens and grassy lawns. Good-looking houses inside neat compounds. It's almost suburban. Outside one of the houses stands Hashim, the farmer who has agreed to show us round today. He is bare-headed, dressed in a simple robe and holds a chain of beads in one hand. He has a strong face and the compact build of someone who might once have been a boxer. With him is one of his sons, Haitham, who has a five-month-old daughter. He is trained in law and speaks English confidently.

Hashim seems a little shy to start with, but once he's with us on his own he reveals a less smooth but equally good grasp of English as his son.

We climb back into the cars and follow him through the town to the fields. There is no evidence here of the destruction which disfigured Mosul and Tikrit and even Samarra, so it comes as quite a shock when we turn the corner of a leafy lane to find ourselves confronted by yet another security checkpoint. This one, however, is very different from any other we've come across. It's more like the local pub. Everyone here seems to know each other. Locals and police are chatting away. There are more bicycles than trucks. The verges around are decorated with spent missile shells, plunged into the ground, their tail-fins painted bright colours. I never thought I'd ever describe an

Iraqi checkpoint as idyllic, but this comes close. Even so the rural police are armed as they are everywhere else, and the delay, though friendly, is rather longer than usual.

Eventually we're cleared to go, and we're soon away from the leafy lanes, and heading into a startlingly different landscape of bone-dry fields and eroded gullies. I learn why we were stopped for so long and why we have been given a four-man police escort. This, like the Makhoul mountains we came through yesterday, is what they would call in Westerns 'bandit country'. Plenty of cover for Daesh fighters to hunker down. Over the last few weeks there have been attacks on police posts.

Hashim is philosophical about it. 'They only come out at night,' he assures me. Far more serious for him is the lack of water. For two

seasons now the rains have failed. He takes me up to the top of a ridge and points out the river bed below. The levels have dropped so far that what is left in the stream is salty and useless. He has had to pay for a generator to bring up water from below ground, but that's expensive, and he can't afford to keep it going for long.

The government is obsessed with oil, he says, yet water supply is far more important for the country. Instead of doing deals with Turkey to secure more water to grow more crops, they spend their time trying to import more food from Iran. He shakes his head. It doesn't make sense.

By now we're into the hottest part of the day. One of the policemen gets out his prayer mat. Another tosses some food to a dog that has been following us all morning. Brown and thin, like the fields.

On the way back to his home, Hashim takes me to a great expanse of what should be wheat fields. No green shoots are showing

here, however, and by now it's too late in the year to plant fresh crops. Another entire harvest has been lost.

It's tragic and deeply ironic. The oldest civilisations in the world grew up here because the land was so fruitful and the wheat so plentiful that there was no need to move into fresh pastures every year. Enough grew to feed everybody and it grew consistently enough to turn nomads into agriculturalists.

I'm aware that Hashim's phone has been ringing insistently. It's his wife who has prepared a meal for us all, wondering when we'll be back.

At the house there is a great spread laid out on the floor, which we eat with our fingers, sitting cross-legged. It's a combination my body embarrassingly resists, and I sit there feeling like a half-collapsed table, which is frustrating as the meal is little short of a banquet. Dolmas, kebabs, falafels, fish, Iraq's national dish mazgouf (grilled Tigris carp), quzi (lamb stuffed with rice, raisins and almonds),

as well as home-grown watermelon, dates and pomegranates. There couldn't be a greater contrast with the grim scenes we saw out in the fields this morning. We ask who we have to thank for all this. His wife and daughter-in-law, Hashim tells us. Can we thank them personally, we ask? Hashim nods. But they are never introduced to us.

We get into a conversation about smoking. Hashim is sixty-two and has a forty-a-day habit which he justifies with dubious statistical evidence based on his family and neighbours.

According to Hashim, all those who have had to have heart surgery have been non-smokers, and all those who haven't have been smokers. Ergo, smoking protects you from heart disease. He trots this out with more sheepishness than triumph, glancing occasionally over his shoulder, leading me to suspect a bit of hen-pecking from the kitchen.

I like Hashim and feel quite honoured when he asks if I'd like to see his workshop. Set back in a tree-filled garden it reminds me of my own father's shed. His tools are neatly laid out. He can make anything there he says.

His two sons, Haitham and Murthan, are both doing well and give me some hope for the future of their country. And Duluiyah seems a good place to live. Before we head back to Baghdad we go down to the banks of the Tigris. There's a road running beside it which isn't litter-strewn. Trees on the promenade are being watered, couples are walking, and there are no guns to be seen. As the sun sets over the river I can see how good life in Iraq might be.

DAY 12

Friday 25th March

OUR SECOND NIGHT AT THE BAGHDAD HOTEL. The change of room has brought on a change of mood. After another minor complication (I was given the keycard to Room 508 which was occupied!), I wake this morning in Room 512 which to my great relief is occupied only by myself. And it's on the best side of the hotel. I can do my morning exercises with a view of the Tigris (or the Dijlah as they call it here) and a Baghdad skyline beyond, dominated by the towering Al Mansour hotel. In 2007 it was the scene of one the most audacious terrorist attacks when a suicide bomber penetrated the tight security and blew the reception area apart, killing himself and twelve others, and wounding eighteen. His target was a group of pro-Western Sunni tribal leaders who had met to discuss how best to deal with the threat posed by al-Qaeda.

Baghdad has experienced terrorist attacks more recently, too. But it has fortunately been spared the systematic destruction that Mosul and Tikrit were forced to endure at the hands of ISIL.

We drive to one of the ferry stations along the river. The water level is low and there's quite a steep drop to the boarding point. A small, businesslike boat, practical and unfussy, takes us across the Tigris to the Old City.

Ahead of us on the far bank is the long multi-arched facade of the Qushla, a handsome late-nineteenth-century Ottoman palace which is now part museum, part public offices. In a country where so many remains of an illustrious past are neglected it's good to see so fine a building in such good condition. We disembark, and climb a few steps up to where a busy crowd mills around a statue, not of a dictator or a politician, but a poet. Abu Tayyib ibn al-Husayn, known as al-Mutanabbi, wrote in the tenth century CE, the period of Abbasid rule when Baghdad was the cultural capital of the Muslim world and scholars came here from near and far to study.

Al-Mutanabbi is celebrated not just with a statue but by a street named after him. That both his statue and his street were given a makeover just over a year ago is an encouraging sign of a cultural renaissance in Baghdad. It's a Friday morning – for Muslims, the busiest day of the week – and Mutanabbi Street is packed with stalls tempting those on their way to and from the mosque with almonds, cashew nuts,

plums and dried prunes from bulging sacks. Fresh pomegranate juice is being turned out with great style, speed and dexterity.

But the street is most renowned for its booksellers – and the Iraqis devour books. I was quoted the line, 'Egyptians write, Lebanese publish, Iraqis read.' Every few yards there are books, often just laid out on carts – not only al-Mutanabbi's poetry but translations of political biographies. I see the lives of Churchill, Hitler and Saddam Hussein displayed side by side. Is this a nostalgia for Great Leaders? A boy offers me some crisp new Iraqi banknotes. Had I not been on camera I might have been tempted as they looked rather beautiful.

We join a queue to get into the handsome Qushla building. Then we make our way to the Qushla Gardens, at the centre of which stands a tall, recently restored clocktower. The gardens are a bit like Speakers' Corner in London – an area where dissent or criticism is allowed to be aired. In the sunshine, by the river, participation seems good-natured.

There is a poetry slam going on at one end of the gardens. Poets come and go, caressing the mikes like well-practised stand-up comedians, vying with each other for the favours of a noisy audience. There is much laughter as fans root for their favourites. The general tone is satirical and anti-government, which might account for the fact that the audience consists mostly of consciously well-dressed young men with immaculate hairstyles. Ammar tells me that there was an embargo on Western goods here, and now it's been lifted, these young men are celebrating choice through their natural sense of display.

There's a good and hopeful atmosphere in the Qushla Gardens today. Lots of people, young and old, men, women and children, mill around; salesmen with pots of fresh coffee and tea and stacks of glasses hanging from their shoulders move amongst the crowd. There's a lack of wariness in the air. In many cities of the world this would just be normal. In Iraq, after all I've seen this past week, it feels encouragingly unusual.

Back in Mutanabbi Street there are reminders of how things have been only too recently. The Shabandar café stands on a busy corner. For over a hundred years it has been a meeting place for writers and intellectuals, for argument, discussion and exchange of ideas. But in 2007 a suicide bomber blew himself up in the street outside. Twenty-six people were killed, among them four sons and a grandson of Mohammed al-Khashali, the proprietor of the Shabandar. No one claimed responsibility but the suspicion is that whoever was behind the attack was seeking to destroy the very values that made Mutanabbi Street so popular – free speech, literacy and open debate.

This morning there is a queue to get in. Despite his dreadful family loss Mohammed al-Khashali still presides over the café, sitting by the door, keeping an eye on the comings and goings. The café has been faithfully restored to what I imagine it must always have been, a place of constant chatter and crowded tables. Windows with panes

of coloured glass give onto the street and songbirds chirrup in cages hung from the ceiling, mimicking the buzz of conversation below. It's lit by traditional glassed lanterns, the light softened by smoke from the hookahs. Copper and silver pots take up any spare space on the shelves, and photos fill the walls, many of them showing figures from the café's and Baghdad's past. One that catches my eye is a reminder that a pattern of violence has dogged the country since its birth. It's a black-and-white framed photo of Faisal II, the last King of Iraq. He sits, smiling, surrounded by his family. In 1958 they were all murdered during the military coup that led to Iraq becoming a republic.

Despite the hubbub, the Shabandar café, with its sense of history and unstoppable bustle, is well worth standing in line for. Once you've found a table it's a very good place to sit and reflect on the fact that free speech can be threatened but not ultimately silenced.

Brief stop-off with Ammar in a quieter side street, then on we

go. Our perambulation takes us up to Al Rashid Street, passing here and there some of the most beautiful old buildings I've seen in Iraq: houses built largely of wood and intricately decorated with wooden balconies projecting out over the crowded streets. They call this style Mashrabiya (or in Basra, Shanasheel). Every touch is delicate and stylish.

Unfortunately, too many of these masterpieces are in bad shape, tilting at angles or literally falling apart. I sense that, without direct intervention from the state, their time has come. The future for Baghdadis is to build big and modern, and many consider these fine houses to be part of a past that is getting in the way of progress. You need the mix, though, and I can think of few better projects than their conservation and restoration. Otherwise these distinctive

examples of Arabic craftsmanship will be gone for ever, and the future is Dubai.

The morning ends with a wonderful lunch at a café with a few tables in a run-down arcade squeezed in between offices. Beautifully tender kebabs, eaten with an abundance of gherkins, onions, olives, tomatoes and great sheets of the most perfectly light oven-fresh bread.

We leave the Old City and walk across the Al-Ahrar bridge to our cars, joining a crowd of shoppers weighed down with heavy bags and facing a long walk home. Salesmen with their goods on wheeled trollies weave among them, speakers on the front of their carts broadcasting their wares electronically, loudly and quite annoyingly. Stalls along the way tempt the shoppers with houseplants or, in one case, circles of fresh-cooked bread as big as medieval shields. In the middle of the

bridge a school party are having a sing-song. What such a scene would be like in the height of summer, when temperatures in Baghdad can touch 50 degrees Celsius, I can't imagine. But today the conditions have been perfect and the Iraqi capital seems to be enjoying itself.

I rather regret having to leave this buzz behind, but this afternoon we are to see a very different side of the city. One not of crowds and gatherings and joining in, but almost exactly the opposite. The Green Zone was created with the explicit purpose of keeping the powerful out of sight. It is completely untypical of the life and spirit of Baghdad, but is probably the only place in the city that anyone outside Iraq has ever heard of. That, of course, is because it is the International Zone, where the largest US embassy in the world, as well as many others, is located, as well as the country's parliament and the president's residence. It's where I've been asked to tea by the British ambassador.

As its name suggests, the Green Zone is a huge tree-lined, park-like area. Hugging the Tigris, and occupying almost four square miles in the middle of the city, it was closed to the public for sixteen years but was finally reopened in 2019. In preparation for this moment, twelve thousand block blast slabs had to be removed.

At the heart of the Green Zone is the vast parade ground created by Saddam Hussein: a long, wide, tarmacked area with rows of seats, terraces, pavilions and saluting areas where Saddam reviewed his troops, often riding a white horse. The most instantly recognisable feature is the Victory Arch, two pairs of crossed swords which straddle it at either end. This was raised to celebrate the end of the bloody Iran–Iraq war of the 1980s – an eight-year struggle triggered by Saddam Hussein's fear that revolutionary Iran might encourage Iraq's Shia majority to rebel against the rule of his Sunni-dominated Ba'ath party and his ambition to become the region's dominant leader. Though the

result of the war was far from decisive, monuments such as the Victory Arch made Saddam, and the Iraqi people, feel that it was and that their sacrifice (a quarter of a million killed on either side) had been worth it. Two years later hubris drew Saddam, high on delusions of grandeur, into invading Kuwait, with disastrous consequences and, for the people of Iraq, yet more suffering.

Like so many of Saddam's grand gestures, they stand, these massive crossed swords, as purposeless as the parade ground which they book-end. There was no one in Iraq able to make them, so the swords, of stainless steel, had to be supplied by a German company. They weigh 24 tons each. The hands and forearms that grasp them weigh 20 tons each and were made by a company based in Basingstoke. They were modelled on Saddam's own hands and his thumbprint was taken to be reproduced, as his signature, on one of them.

In 2007 there was a move to dismantle the swords but nothing came of it and, a few years later, the Victory Arch was actually restored. It may have no use, other than to serve as a memorial for those who died for their country in Saddam's wars, but it is a striking piece of design and craftsmanship and, rising as it does 130 feet into the air, it has become one of Baghdad's most distinctive, if equivocal, landmarks.

This afternoon, there's no one around but ourselves and a security detachment, who want to have a photo taken with me. We proceed on our way past all sorts of government buildings, including one which discreetly announces itself as the *'Iraqi Anti-Corruption Academy'*. There must be plenty of work to do there.

Finally we reach the gates of the British embassy. Here we're back in high-security mode. We have to submit to full checks before we can come in off the road, and once inside, we're into a series of twisting high-walled chicanes, before entering a yard where all our bags have to

be removed from the vehicles, laid in a line on the ground and exhaustively sniffed at by dogs and physically checked by humans before we can re-pack and move a few yards closer to the residence itself, tucked away as it is at the heart of the labyrinth.

Mark, ambassador for the last three months, apologises for all the precautions. Touch wood the British embassy has never been attacked – the Americans are the main target. But it must be a bit like living in a bunker, I suggest, and I wonder just how long it will be before Iraq is considered safe enough for some of these walls to be taken down.

He shows me into a large living room. As in most embassies the rooms are never inhabited for long enough by any one individual to reflect that person's lifestyle. They're tasteful but a bit corporate. On one wall is a painting by Gertrude Bell, one of the founders of modern Iraq. She was many things: a brilliant scholar, an archaeologist, mountaineer and traveller. She was a close friend of Lawrence of Arabia, and it was their knowledge of, and attraction to, Arab culture that proved so vital in deciding how the Middle East should be rebuilt after the collapse of the Ottoman empire. She remained close to the country she helped create, and died in Baghdad in 1926. Why there hasn't been a film of her life starring Meryl Streep I don't know.

The ambassador doesn't drink, having married a Muslim woman and converted to the faith, but I'm served a G and T as we sit out on a cool patio and talk about what must be one of the Foreign Office's trickier diplomatic assignments. Mark has close contact with all the main players in Iraqi politics but I sense his frustration at the difficulties of governance in a country still divided by small parties, oppositional militias and quarrelling sectarian interests. He tries, as a good diplomat should, to be convincingly optimistic about the future. The fact remains, though, that we have almost certainly seen more of the country in the last ten days than he has been allowed or able to visit since he arrived here.

The last assignment for me today is supper with Sara, a young Iraqi woman of great poise and confidence, mostly acquired during time spent in Malaysia. She is a bio-physicist and speaks several languages, all of which sounds intimidating but she's very easy to talk to. She is introducing me to a restaurant where they serve the national dish, mazgouf. We're a few yards from the Tigris, from which the fish must be taken, and at this restaurant they take pride in serving it the traditional way.

We go round the back where the fish, a variety of carp, are removed from a tank, killed, then cut along the back and spread out.

Then, rather spectacularly, they're gutted, salted and grilled up against a frame of sticks around a fire of pomegranate wood. Skill and judgement are required to keep the fire burning at just the right temperature and at just the right distance from the fish. When it's judged to be perfectly done, the mazgouf is taken from the fire on a wooden pitchfork. It all looks very medieval and probably is.

Sara and I take a table in the garden. Though it's quite chilly now, we have no option, as the interior of the restaurant is reserved for men only. It's quite atmospheric out here. The tall tower of the Hotel Palestine rises across the road, and the night air is enriched by a chorus of squawks and screeches from the restaurant's parrot and parakeet enclosure.

I think that the ambassador's gin and tonic has begun to affect my concentration and I find the immaculately prepared mazgouf almost impossible to eat. Consumption, it seems, is as complex as preparation. The bones, like the concrete walls of the embassy compound, have to be carefully negotiated and the flesh retrieved from only certain parts of the fish. Sara quietly and efficiently helps me out, and as our long day draws to an end I feel as if I'm in a care home.

Back at the Baghdad Hotel the day is not quite over. Though I'm now happily ensconced in Room 512, I find that one of my jackets must still be in a cupboard in Room 323. But there are now other guests in there. However, after a commando raid by the helpful staff I am at last reunited with my jacket, and Room 323 is no longer anything to do with me.

I wouldn't go on about it, but it's things like this that keep crew morale up. I can hear their laughter now.

THIS MORNING I'M GOING TO BABYLON. NOW THERE'S a sentence I never thought I'd write. In historical terms, Baghdad is a baby compared to Babylon. Work on the capital only began in 762 CE. The glory days of Babylon, which my guidebook reminds me is described in the Book of Revelations as 'Babylon the Great, Mother of harlots and the abominations of the earth', were nearly three thousand years earlier. Then it went into a decline before re-emerging, briefly, under Nebuchadnezzar II as one of the most magnificent cities on earth.

Its years of greatness were interspersed with invasions and regular sackings. A century after the Persian King Cyrus II seized it in the sixth century BCE, Herodotus could describe it wonderingly as 'a vast city . . . with sides nearly fourteen miles long and a circuit of some fifty-six miles . . . it surpasses in splendour any city of the known world.' The Greeks rated the Hanging Gardens of Babylon as one of the Seven Wonders of the World. Yet when Alexander arrived a couple of

hundred or so years later he found little left. He attempted some recon-struction of the great temple, but died before the task was finished, and was buried in Babylon in 323 BCE. A few hundred years later it was a village. By the end of the first millennium of our era it had been abandoned.

Now, despite its turbulent history, the great name of Babylon is a barely discernible dot on the map, a tourist site upstaged by neigh-bours like Karbala, Hillah and Najaf, all flourishing because of their religious significance.

We come upon Babylon quite abruptly after a ninety-minute drive south from Baghdad. Because it's no longer inhabited, there's no surrounding settlement to tell us we've arrived. Instead, we're suddenly confronted by a tall arched gateway standing out from the desert, with two towers on either side, surfaced with bricks glazed as blue as the sky and decorated with relief sculptures of lions, bulls and a mythical dragon called the mushussu. This is the Ishtar Gate and it is very fine and striking. But it's not the real thing. The original is in a museum in Berlin.

I try my best not to be disappointed with Babylon. I look carefully at the limited exhibition in the courtyard beyond the Ishtar Gate, but don't glean much. I walk up onto a viewing platform and admire the long, angled brick walls that stretch away in front of me and try to let my imagination overcome the knowledge that most of these walls were built in my lifetime by Saddam Hussein who, seeing himself a Nebuchadnezzar for his times, ordered his architects to restore the old walls of the city. They've done them well, with the size and colour of the small muddy-brown, almost yellow bricks matching the original. I know that because I'm accompanied by Dr Haider, a most amiable and interesting archaeologist and an expert on Babylon, who points out

that the metre or so of old bricks at the foot of the restored walls do date from Nebuchadnezzar's time. The scale of the palace is immense and I walk into courtyard after reconstructed courtyard. A series of wide empty spaces but enough of them to suggest how busy a place this must once have been.

Just as I'm feeling admiration rather than thrill Dr Haider shows me something that makes the whole visit worthwhile. Down some steps, fenced off by workmen, is the original site of the Ishtar Gate. We're given permission to go down and take a look. Here in the Processional Way, the walls are rougher, they don't have the glow of their modern counterparts – but they are the real thing. And all along them are the reliefs of the various animals, real and mythical, the likenesses of which we have seen displayed on the remodelled Ishtar Gate.

I can't go far along this magical passage, paved with the same slabs as Nebuchadnezzar would have seen, without catching my breath at the closeness of ancient history.

I'm jolted back to the present as a crane swings some masonry high over the walls. It's being operated on behalf of an American team continuing the endless task of excavating the Babylonian empire.

The key to the fate of these old civilisations was often down to quirks of geography. Because the lands they occupied were low-lying and bordered by two big rivers, they were at the mercy of the water flows. Too little and there would be drought. Too much and there could be spectacular flooding. Here in Babylon the Euphrates, flowing out of Syria in the west, edges closer to the Tigris, increasing the risk of flood. The story of Noah's Ark is thought by some to have been handed

down from the great flood described in the story of Gilgamesh, the Sumerian hero, written around 2100 BCE. When the water flows are steady, regular and generous this is still a potentially rich land.

I think of this as we drive a mile or so west to a present-day palace built by Saddam Hussein overlooking the Euphrates. Thousands of people were employed here and the building took over five years to complete. This huge folly has been spared the destruction wreaked on his Tikrit palaces, but has suffered a different kind of humiliation. Left empty and only lightly guarded, it is open to the public who are free to wander amongst the rooms he spent so much money decorating and dressing. And they have left their own decorations. Every wall, every pillar, every staircase is scrawled with graffiti. This truly is Hubris Hall. Rubbish has gathered on fine marble floors, blown up against walls lined with the finest Moroccan wood. When the American forces arrived here in 2003, they used its grandest room as a basketball court.

A few miles west of Babylon is the city of Karbala, one of the holiest cities of the Muslim world. A prime destination for religious tourists, it brings some two billion dollars a year into Iraq, the second

biggest earner after oil. A battle took place here in 680 CE in which the two grandsons of the prophet Muhammad, Imam Husayn and Imam Abbas, were killed. They are both revered by Shia Muslims, and pilgrims come here, many of them from Iran, to pay their respects and to bring gifts or donations. The two mosques, one for Husayn and the other for Abbas, exude wealth, with shining gold domes and glittering, almost Vegas-like interiors. On the approach to Husayn's mosque, with its entrance the size of a railway station, there's a wrecked building on a corner of the square outside; concrete floors hanging at crazy angles, piping and cabling exposed, twisted metal and dust rising. It looks like so many we saw in Mosul and Tikrit. But here it's not war damage that is to blame; the building's being cleared away to make even more space for religious tourists, the lifeblood of the city.

We remove our shoes, hand them over and make our way inside. There are hundreds of worshippers, some kneeling to Mecca, others making straight for the huge golden casket which contains Imam Husayn's remains, others reading the Quran. I see one man simply sitting cross-legged by a pillar, sobbing.

Every now and then coffins are rushed in on the shoulders of lamenting families and laid on the floor to be blessed before they go to the Shia cemetery at the nearby holy city of Najaf.

An army of staff is required to run the shrine. Twenty thousand are on the payroll, I'm told. Vacuum cleaners are constantly being pushed across the carpets, while security men try to avoid congestion by moving people on with ostrich-feather switches. Walkie-talkies are everywhere. I'm used to a very strictly organised form of worship. In this mosque everything is more spontaneous and seemingly less structured. All human life, and death, is here.

We're back on the road to Baghdad as it's getting dark, and later than our security escort like us to travel. For many miles beyond Karbala, green neon lights in the shape of palm trees decorate the palm trees.

DAY 14

اليوم الرابع عشر

Sunday 27th March

WE'RE DUE TO LEAVE BAGHDAD THIS EVENING, AND
as I draw back my curtains I take in the panorama of Iraq's capital one
last time. The Tigris is serene in the sunshine, her surface mirroring
the city around her. In the far distance I can pick out a Ferris wheel,
and the Victory Arch, the morning sun catching the tips of the crossed
swords. Further to the west is the tall, strikingly elegant Central
Bank of Iraq tower. It was designed by Zaha Hadid, who was born in
Baghdad. At nearly 600 feet high it embodies the spirit of a city on the
cusp of a revival, ready to take its place once again at the heart of the
Middle East.

There are other signs that Baghdad is sprucing itself up. Not just
with sleek new buildings but with newly paved, well-lit riverside prom-
enades and impressive housing developments.

But the future of Iraq lies in the hands of the generation still at
school, and this morning we're driving out to meet some of them.

I find that every journey in Iraq is full of conflicting images,
and today as we drive across town, my morning's sunny optimism is

tempered by the sight of black-clad police with riot shields deployed on the streets and at roundabouts. No one seems to know what threat has brought them out in such numbers. There's speculation that it could be to do with possible crowd trouble ahead of the upcoming presidential elections. Iraq is a parliamentary democracy, and though the presidency is a largely ceremonial role, the president is the one who chooses the prime minister – an altogether more important office. You can't have one without the other.

With some difficulty we find the school, tucked away in a featureless suburb of the city. The ministry with which a visit like this has to be cleared has doubtless chosen it carefully for us, as this is a special school for high-achieving children. From the age of nine the brightest are plucked from schools all over Baghdad and brought here to mix with equally clever pupils through to their teens.

There are conditions attached to this elite education, however. The curriculum is heavily science-based. They do a lot of chemistry and physics, and it is obligatory that they enter the medical profession. Iraqi doctors are in demand around the world, but it seems odd that if you want to become an engineer, you must first pass your medical exams.

Despite this being a school for top children, it's not in great shape. The air-con is intermittent, the windows dirty and the table-tennis table is covered with a layer of sticky dust. Considering the emphasis on chemistry and physics, there are very few lab facilities. There is a small garden outside, uncared for.

When we arrive, it's break time, and the children welcome us with noisy enthusiasm. Eloquent, articulate and eager, they mill around us. They have six lessons of English a week. They've never met anyone from outside Iraq and they have so many questions they want to ask.

I'm impressed by the children, but not so much by the administration. The head teacher seems reluctant to engage with us. Ammar says men like him are put in place by the government. They're not expected to do anything very exciting or dynamic; they're simply there to make sure no one else does anything exciting or dynamic. I begin to understand why some of the Iraqis we have met have complained about what they see as a national malaise of heavy-handed bureaucracy, smothering initiative.

One can only hope that the energy and effervescence of the children we spoke to will survive into adulthood. If not, then it's hard to be overly optimistic about the future.

It's one o'clock now. The end of the school day, and the children are waving goodbye before being picked up by their parents. In Baghdad traffic their journeys home could easily take two hours. I don't see a school bus anywhere.

From the school we make our way to Baghdad Central station where, all being well, we'll take the sleeper service to Basra tonight. In terms of size and scale it can compete with the best in the world. It's also one of the most beautiful buildings in the city. The architect was a Scot, J. M. Wilson, who had worked with Lutyens in Delhi. He went to great lengths to reflect the history and culture of Iraq in his design. The tall, colonnaded entrance is flanked by two soaring clocktowers, with all the grace and strength of Assyrian pylons. Both clocks show different times. Neither is right.

Wide steps lead up to a stunning interior. Light streams in from a dome high above from which a massive chandelier complete with opaque glass bowl is suspended. Supporting the roof is a series of tall, fluted columns in the shape of palm trees. Everything about the design celebrates the scale and character of Iraq.

Sadly, this has not been reciprocated by today's railway company. Signs at long-closed counters show what the country's railway network must once have been like. *'Booking for Train to Mosul'* above one counter, *'Baghdad–Syria'* at another. Tucked away near the toilets is a display board headed *'Table of Iraqi Railway Projects'*. The list of twelve schemes is impressive, including Mosul to Turkey and an Iraq–Jordan connection. A closer look reveals none of them has been completed. Half of them have reached the stage of *'Updating design'* and two others have got as far as *'Proposed'*. Only one is actually *'Under Construction'*.

Name of Project	Current Stage of Project	Length of Main Route of Project /km	Cost of Project (M. US Dollar)	Design Speed for trains (km/hr)	Design Axle Load (Tone)	Annual Design Transport Capacity
Mussaib – Karbala – Najaf – Samawa	Design is Completed	246 km Double Track	2640	250 - Passengers 140 - Freights	25	(6 M.) Passengers, (2 M.) Tones of Freights
Loop Railway line around Baghdad City	Updating Design	140 km Double Track	2429	200 - Passengers 140- Freights	25	(23M.) Passengers, (46M.) Tones of Freights
Baghdad – Ba'qoba – Kirkuk – Erbil – Mosul	Updating Design	555 km Double Track	8674	250 - Passengers 140 Freights	25	(6M.) Passengers, (20M.) Tones of Freights
Baghdad – Kut – Amara – Basra and Kut Nasiriya – Basra- Um Qasr	Updating Design	910 km Double Track	13739	250 - Passengers 140 - Freights	25	(14M.) Passengers, (35M.) Tones of Freights
Mosul – Duhok – Zakho – Turkey	Updating Design	167 km Double Track	2607	200 - Passengers 140 - Freights	25	(1M.) Passengers, (55M.) Tones of Freights
Basra – Pao	Detailed Design	101 km Double Track	1489	140 - Passengers 100 - Freights	25	(1M.) Passengers, (70M.) Tones of Freights
Kirkuk – Sulaimaniya	Detailed Design	118 km Double Track	1855	200 - Passengers 140 - Freights	25	(1.5M.) Passengers, (6M.) Tones of Freights
Karbala – Ramadi	Updating Design	132 km Double Track	1089	250 - Passengers 140 - Freights	25	(3M.) Passengers, (36M.) Tones of Freights
Kut – Ba'qoba	Proposed	250 km Double Track	3760	250 - Passengers, 140 - Freights	25	(6M.) Passengers, (20M.) Tones of Freights
Iraq – Jordan Railway connection (Ramadi – Terebil)	Preliminary Designs	420 km Double Track	5066	160- 250 –Passengers 120 Freights	25	(2.5M.) Passengers, (12M.) Tones of Freights
Development & Reconstruction of Existing Baghdad – Basra & Baghdad – Mosul Railway lines to make Double Track lines	Under Construction	1135 km Double Track	3000	120 - Passengers 70 - Freights	25	(4M.) Passengers, (24M.) Tones of Freights
Electrification & Signaling & Telecommunication & Purchasing of New Rolling Stock Fleet	Proposed		10000	According to the speed of each project		

Total Length of Iraqi Railways Network will be (10000) km, Ten thousands Kilometers including Stations Yards lines.
Total Cost for construction of these projects with cost of lands acquisition is (60) Billions of US Dollar.

The fact is that whereas in most capitals the mainline station is
the hub of city life, a place of comings and goings and constant activity,
Baghdad Central is the opposite. Quiet as a library, it's an oasis of
tranquillity in an incessantly rowdy city. Only three trains a week use
it. One of them is the sleeper service to Basra on which, all being well,
we leave tonight.

The train itself looks smart enough. It's made up of old Chinese
high-speed stock. It leaves at seven o'clock but no one is allowed
through until a half-hour before. On the way through the barrier we
pass beneath a large photograph of Muqtada al-Sadr and his father, a
reminder that the train will be taking us into the Shia heartlands of

southern Iraq. Muqtada and his Shiite alliance formed a powerful force of resistance during the American occupation, and currently constitute the biggest bloc in the Iraqi parliament.

Before we can board the train, all the passengers – and I would think there are two or three hundred of us – have to lay their bags out in a line, which is then searched by sniffer dogs. The railway officials are happy for us to film this reassuring picture of security but as soon as the search is over, and there is a mad stampede for the train, Jaimie is asked very firmly to switch his camera off.

'Don't film the chaos, please!'

Being on a train anywhere is a small thrill for me, but being on the Baghdad–Basra sleeper ticks all the boxes from exciting to exotic to eccentric. My compartment is clean and well equipped, with a fridge, a basin, lots of cupboards and a neat little reading light. And we pull out on time.

We're not going all the way to Basra. We shall be getting off at Nasiriyah at 2.30 tomorrow morning, which means there's not much prospect of a good night's sleep. There's no restaurant car, so in the spirit of a midnight feast we gather in my compartment to eat the food we've brought, together with a smuggled bottle of wine, before splitting up for a hopeful few hours' sleep.

Hopes largely dashed. A wash before bed would have been nice, but there's no water from the taps and no soap in the dispenser. Though the ride is reasonably smooth, the glaring ceiling light in my compartment comes on about midnight and can't be turned off.

Looking out of the window is not much of an option, as the glass is smeared and greasy.

The train we all went on in North Korea was like a Pullman compared to this.

DAY 15
اليوم الخامس عشر
Monday 28th March

IT'S 1.30 IN THE MORNING. I'M WOKEN FROM WHATEVER short sleep I might have had as we are expected to arrive in Nasiriyah within the half-hour. Very few people get off at this stop. Once we've disembarked, the train gives a muffled hoot and carries on its way to Basra, leaving a great silence behind.

Outside the anonymous station there is an unexpected surprise: a small green steam engine on a plinth. It offers a reassuring sight in what could be quite a sinister atmosphere. Our drivers wait to take us on to our hotel. Voices are muted as we load our gear. All anyone wants now is a proper bed in a room that doesn't move.

Nasiriyah, 225 miles south of Baghdad, is the fourth-biggest city in Iraq, yet merits barely two pages in my guidebook, which talks of its 'dissident reputation for unrest'. I get no sense of an urban presence as we drive through empty streets lined with the usual straggle of unkempt houses. We cross a bridge over the Euphrates, pass a short way alongside the river and there, on a corner, is the Al-Zaitoon hotel, our home for the next two nights.

It's compact and recently built; but all that matters to us is that our rooms are ready. It's close to three o'clock when I switch my light off.

When I wake it's nine o'clock. I've slept comfortably and after the numbness of our arrival last night I feel my curiosity aroused, in a good way. Southern Iraq is, I feel, going to be a very different experience from anywhere I've been so far. Well, I'm right. As I draw back my curtains, I instinctively recoil. One of the panes has a bullet hole in it. This certainly arouses my curiosity. How recently was my room fired on? How deeply have I been sleeping? Are they still out there? Moving to one side of the window I check the street outside. An old man in a white robe and carrying a plastic bag shuffles by. The Euphrates moves sluggishly with him, its banks strewn with a muddy mess of builders' debris.

At breakfast everything is normal, and we enjoy our meal of boiled egg, watermelon, honey from the honeycomb and bread. There are no reports of any other window damage. I must accentuate the positive. In any case we have come to Nasiriyah, not so much to dwell on the present, but to take the opportunity to see one of the world's great monuments, and one of the greatest riches of Iraq's past. Only a few miles outside the city is the ziggurat at Ur. Built over four thousand years ago, around the time of Stonehenge, it is one of those enormous constructions that has a legendary, slightly unreal quality. I can't help wondering whether something of such scale and power really does exist, or whether artists' impressions in childhood encyclopedias have created a false picture in my mind. Today I'll find out.

We drive for about half an hour, out of Nasiriyah and into the desert. A long, straight road past a generating station and a forest of pylons. A bare, unconsoling landscape. Not for the first time, I feel as if I'm in a Western. Then, appearing simultaneously out of the heat, like a dual mirage, are the curved metal roofs of an airbase and, almost close enough to seem part of it, the unmistakable silhouette of the ziggurat, with its mighty bulk and tall, powerfully angled walls. Ancient and modern.

There are a few huts and a car park set back from the ziggurat and connected to it by a duckboard walkway. There had been some doubt as to whether we should be allowed to climb it, but access has been granted. As I approach this colossal structure I can pick out more detail. Sheer walls lean in a pyramid shape. It's estimated that 420,000 bricks would have been needed to build it, all bound together with the local and plentiful bitumen. A long stone staircase ascends to a wide, flat platform, a hundred feet off the ground, with two other approaches sweeping down on either side. The ziggurat, part of a temple complex and a shrine to the moon god, has a presence equalling that of any of the pyramids, but unlike its Egyptian counterparts it has terraces on different levels and no network of chambers inside. It has no tourists, either.

Its sheer size is impressive, but so are the engineering and building skills that must have been mastered to keep it all together. Excavations nearby reveal that those who built it lived in mud-walled huts.

I climb the stairs and explore the view from the top. A fiercely gusting wind whips around me, sending clouds of swirling sand against the walls. When built it must all have been very different. The Euphrates floodplain would have been less extensive, the ziggurat closer to the sea. And it would have been at the heart of a much busier and more fertile place – the Sumerian city of Ur. After the fall of Saddam Hussein, ex-soldier, writer and sometime Conservative politician Rory Stewart spent time in this province as Deputy Governor for the Coalition Provisional Authority – the occupying forces. He wrote an eloquent speech delivered at an official function held on the ziggurat itself. He placed the great building at '... the centre of the world's first civilisation. Within one hundred metres of us lie cuneiform tablets written in an alphabet invented here five thousand years ago ... A little further on and we come to the oldest law court in the world and the house where Abraham was born.'

What he couldn't say publicly at that time is that, as in Babylon, Saddam Hussein had restored much of what we see today.

There are excavations under way, which offer exciting prospects, but there doesn't seem to be a lot of investment going in and it will be well into the future before all the secrets of Ur are revealed.

Back at the hotel there are three power cuts in quick succession, and the wind whistles through the bullet hole.

DAY 16
Tuesday 29th March

AS WE PACK UP TO LEAVE THE AL-ZAITOON, I WALK ACROSS the road to pay my respects to the Euphrates. It flows out of a city rebuilding itself, repairing the damage it sustained. It's frustrating that, apart from the ziggurat, the evidence of the glorious past of Ur of the Chaldees is buried somewhere, beneath the rubble of the present.

I climb into the car. I can leave Nasiriyah with some satisfaction. At least I've achieved a childhood ambition to see a ziggurat, and to tread the sands where Ur once stood, even if I did have to put my imagination into overdrive.

Nasiriyah by day is a big, lively town with its own formidable rush hour, which we negotiate slowly. One feature of the roads here and throughout southern Iraq is the profusion of posters of Shia heroes such as Muqtada al-Sadr, Ayatollah Khomeini, and the photogenic silver-bearded twosome of Iranian General Qassim Soleimani and Iraqi militia leader Abu Mahdi al-Mohandes, both of whom were assassinated by the Americans at Baghdad airport just over two years ago. Gone, but certainly not forgotten. We are into conservative Shia Iraq here and there are no helpful English translations on the signs and billboards. I feel oddly uneasy, very much an outsider.

I ask my driver about the black flags I see with increasing frequency, and which remind me uncomfortably of the flags carried by ISIS convoys as they swept into towns and villages. I'm told that these could not be more different. They are black as a sign of respect for the death of the Prophet's grandson Husayn, thirteen hundred years ago. And the occasional red flags? They're in memory of his brother Ahmad. The flags, and little huts for overnight refuge, are there to encourage those doughty pilgrims who make the 300-mile journey from Basra to the shrine at Karbala by foot.

Down here in the south, religion has claimed the roadside.

We're now witnessing the last acts of the journey of the Tigris and Euphrates to the sea. And in their very late stages they've created something quite spectacular. It's a whole unique environment: a wide area of marshland, formed over the years by the deposits from the rivers which pushed back the sea and created a unique and constantly changing riverine habitat; one which has been settled for many thousands of years by those generally lumped together as Marsh Arabs. In

the 1940s and '50s that most intrepid of English travellers, Wilfred Thesiger, lived among them, and I've been preparing myself for our visit by reading his friend Gavin Maxwell's account of their time together in the marshes, *A Reed Shaken by the Wind*. It's an affectionate portrait of an idiosyncratic community, but some of the observations have left me distinctly queasy. Especially on the digestion front. Quoting the Arab proverb, 'Eat like a camel and be the first to finish', Maxwell explains that every meal 'is, indeed, a sort of eating race, and each man crams himself feverishly, in a silence unbroken save for champing jaws and the occasional belch'. His description of the content of the cuisine makes it sound pretty alarming, too. Sheep's heads cooked on a buffalo-dung fire, for instance. 'Pieces of flesh from the ear, the hair still attached, are esteemed a delicacy.'

Saddam Hussein, accusing the Marsh Arabs of aiding and abet-
ting the enemy in the Iran–Iraq war, retaliated by draining the marshes,
deliberately depriving their inhabitants of their homes and livelihoods. In
the 1950s there were close to half a million living in the marshes. When
Saddam destroyed their way of life, their numbers dropped to twenty
thousand. They've now recovered somewhat, but only to forty thousand.

After Saddam's fall the waters flowed again and this extraordinary
ecosystem began to re-establish itself. Though it is far from fully
restored, it now, according to a government body grandly titled the
Centre for Iraqi Marshes and Wetlands, covers an area of nearly four
thousand square miles.

Our time in Iraq is running out, which makes every interruption
even more frustrating. On the road from Nasiriyah we're stopped in
the middle of nowhere at a checkpoint manned by a single guard. And
he's in no hurry to let us through whilst he seeks confirmation that we
are who we say we are. Forty-five minutes later we're on our way. The
landscape is changing quite dramatically. The long, straight road is now
running alongside watery reedbeds. Heathland has become marshland.
It's not unlike east Suffolk.

At a small town we embark in narrow, sharp-nosed canoes that
will take us up through the canals into the marshes.

With us is Azzam, a vocal enthusiast and expert on the way of
life here. As we speed out onto the water he shouts to me over the
noise of the outboard. The main problem these days, he explains, is
water distribution. The survival of the marshes depends on the rain that
falls hundreds of miles to the north in Turkey and Kurdistan, making it
no longer just a question of climate but of politics, too. Without that
water the plants cannot grow, the birds have nothing to feed on, and
the whole cycle of birth and re-birth is disrupted. Our river journey

comes full circle. The fate of the Marsh Arabs and the snows of Turkey inextricably linked.

The canal system in the marshes is like a road network: main high-ways, up which our wiry, aged boatman can squeeze the throttle and, leading off them, narrower access channels. Since the reeds that line them can be damaged by the wash from the boat's propellors, we slow down, giving me a chance to take in something I've seen so little of in Iraq thus far: its wildlife. Flocks of graceful white herons skim the reeds, and kingfishers dart about. We put in at a small island only a few yards square to which we're welcomed by a noisy herd of geese. A family of ten people lives here, together with the geese and a lot of chickens.

And that's not all. When I wander into the larger of the two reed-built houses a dozen heads turn towards me. They're water buffaloes, precious enough to the family to have them sharing the accommodation.

Sabah Thamer Htaiht, the head of the family, is a young man, solemn and passionate about their life on the island. When Saddam drained the marshes, the family moved to Samarra, two hundred miles away. He and his father had to take menial jobs to survive and were deeply unhappy there.

Though his father is now very sick, he's much happier to be back in the marshes on the island where he was born and where his family have lived for so long. The son shows me round. The houses are made entirely from reeds and bulrushes, and are measured by the number of arches they need to support the roof. One is a 'bachelor hut', of five arches, which is where visitors stay. The family all live in the ten-arch hut. With the buffaloes, I assume.

It looks idyllic but all is not well. They make their living largely from fishing, but for two years now the spring rains have failed and the water has become less clean and the fish fewer. He doesn't believe the government are doing much to protect their livelihoods. There is a living to be made from cutting and selling the reeds, but a day's work would earn you only about twenty dollars. His children are educated at home. Getting to the nearest school is too much of a hassle. Surprisingly enough he sees some hope in tourism. He has had visitors to stay here and there is a growing appetite for people to know more about life on the islands.

Those who live among the marshes have always been skilful, self-sufficient and independent. They're bloody-minded and proud of it. Which is why Saddam Hussein came for them.

I hope they survive here. It is a way of life very much in harmony with nature, so much more attractive than the noisy, dirty, hot streets of the cities.

As we leave I ask Azzam what he thinks the future might be. He, too, sees some hope in tourism – that visitors will want to come to this unique world and be welcomed by people like Sabah. The water shortage can be partly alleviated by reverse osmosis which can turn seawater into drinking water. But he is not hopeful that the government cares enough to face up to the Marsh Arabs' problems. The money is there but it disappears into so many pockets before being spent where it's needed. He shakes his head in frustration. Iraq, he says grimly, is a kleptocracy.

No time for sheep's head as we have to move on, scudding swiftly back down the canals, passing several equally swift canoes carrying stacks of fresh-cut reeds. I'm aware that the marshes and the people who live there are constantly adapting. The fact that we can race along at 20 knots or more is already a big change from the days when the boats were punted about with long poles and Wilfred Thesiger marvelled at 'the stillness of a world that never knew an engine'.

We drive to Al-Qurnah, an ordinary looking town but significant for us because it is here that the Tigris, which we've followed for nearly a thousand miles, meets the Euphrates. Together they become the rather less poetic Shatt al-Arab, which carries their waters the last 120 miles to the Persian Gulf.

There is a fan-shaped viewing platform thoughtfully provided for those who want to stand at the confluence. The two rivers look exhausted. I can't easily reconcile the sluggish Tigris I see here, confined within dried and cracked banks, with the majestic river I saw flowing under the Ten Eye bridge at Diyarbakir two weeks ago.

There are limited visitor facilities. A few plastic chairs, a small café with a Father Christmas on one of the shelves. Music plays from speakers and a group of four young men is concentrating hard on a game of dominoes. Occasionally someone will walk up to be photographed at the point where the Tigris and Euphrates, the Dijlah and the al-Furat, come together, but it's hardly a tourist destination. This could be because there is a rival attraction in a public garden nearby. Bible stories are never far away in Iraq, so perhaps it shouldn't come as a surprise, except to those who've seen it, that Al-Qurnah is thought to be the site of the Garden of Eden, and an ancient tree in this small park where the rivers join is thought to be the successor to the Tree of Knowledge.

It is less than impressive. A bleached white bark, encased in a marble base and surrounded by a chain hung from green and white metal posts, it looks to have been dead for quite a while. A sign alongside proclaims it, in Arabic and English, as 'Adam's Tree'. It has an accompanying inscription: '*In this blessed area where Tigris and Euphrates meet a tree was honoured by the visit of our master Ibrahim al Khaleel peace be upon him in 2000 PC* [sic]. *He praged* [sic] *and said here a tree will grow which is similar to our father Adams* [sic] *tree.*'

As we used to say at school, it's a bit of a swizz really. There are families in this part of the garden and people picnicking on the patches of grass, but none of them seem particularly interested in the Tree of Knowledge. I can't help but think what some smart operator back home would make of the site of the Garden of Eden.

From Al-Qurnah it's only a short way to Basra, Iraq's second-biggest, and second-best-known, city. Like Baghdad it has, for me, a touch of childhood fascination about it. After all, it was the home of Sinbad the Sailor. But somehow I don't feel as comfortable here as I did in Baghdad. All the checkpoints, walls, lamp posts, fences, billboards are covered in the now familiar Shia faces, the clerics, the martyrs, those alive or dead. I can usually read the streets of any city, and feel that although I'm in someone else's country there's always common ground. But here, bombarded by all these male faces and the stern, judgemental attitudes they seem to represent, I feel like a fish out of water.

We embark on a late-evening visit to some of the streets of the Old City. Bathed in the golden glow of the evening sun, this should have been the perfect time to enjoy the old houses which the Jewish, Christian and Muslim trading families built around the canals many years ago, and which earned Basra the name Venice of the East.

Many of them remain and you can't help but be dazzled by the craftsmanship of the finely crafted bays decorated with intricate lattice-work and ornate stained glass. They are some of the most attractive urban buildings I've ever seen. But that makes their dismal state of preservation all the harder to accept. In one street the old houses give on to canals, accessed by individual bridges. These bridges seem to have been used by fly-tippers to sling any kind of rubbish and food waste into the canals, where it lies, rotting and uncollected, on the surface of the water. Some have been half-restored, and there are signs of a UNESCO presence, but the prevailing feeling is that the city of Basra wishes to spend its money on the future rather than the past.

What I had hoped might be a highlight of my visit to Basra only compounds my feeling of dislocation. I feel a bit like those old houses – as if I'm not really welcome here.

The hotel is big and my room comfortable, and there are no holes in the window, but the buffet is a soulless meal in a soulless space. The staff are pleasant enough, though only minimally helpful. It's as if the whole place is in a daze. Or maybe it's just me at the end of a long journey.

DAY 17

الـيَـوُم الـسّـابِـع عَشَـر

Wednesday 30th March

OUT EARLY TO FILM BY THE RIVER. I FEEL MUCH BETTER today. Spruced up by a shower and a night's sleep. Last night, as we arrived in grinding traffic and after a long day in the marshes, I had no real sense of the place, and the time I spent in old Basra was just depressing. This morning, observing a wide, paved corniche being laid along the waterside, I can see where some of the country's oil revenues are going. It shouldn't be an alternative to the restoration of the old city but it's impressive in scope and scale. The only thing that's missing is any shelter from the sun. For the first time on the journey I feel sunshine strong enough to avoid, and it's only March. By July the average temperature in Basra will be 46 degrees Celsius. I seek out a narrow line of shade from a newly planted palm tree. Hiding from the heat like this reminds me of my travels in the Sahara, and makes me long for the cool mountains of Kurdistan.

The end of our journey is in sight.

Today we shall follow the Tigris and Euphrates on their last lap
to the sea. We struggle out of Basra, ducking and diving through traffic,
crunching to a halt in long jams, through which pass men and women
with unbearably pained faces, hands outstretched towards the windows.
I notice that our driver always gives them some change.

Once clear of the city, as Iraq narrows to its 36-mile coastline,
the terrain is, on one side, increasingly apocalyptic. A landscape of
mudflats and salt-pans. On the other, eastern side, where the Shatt
al-Arab runs, there is more greenery and a glimpse of a gold-domed
mosque. That's Iran.

Then, without warning, silos rise out of the wilderness with lines of heavily laden vehicles crawling towards them. Late in our journey it may be, but at the very end of the country we have come upon the biggest construction project in Iraq. At Al Faw, once just a small-time fishing town, work has been going on for the past eight years to create a new port from scratch, one of the largest and most up to date in the Middle East. A port system so huge and complex, it'll be another twenty years before it's fully operational. As we drive into the work site, a signboard announces – in English and Arabic – that they've already completed 'The Longest Breakwater in the World'. It's in *Guinness World Records*, I'm told. Seventeen kilometres long. That's over ten miles.

I never expected that some of the last people I'd meet in Iraq would be from places like Frome and Warrington, but some of the supervisory work on this mammoth operation is being done by Brits. James, who's head of security – 'I'm controlling over a hundred kilo-metres, which is a bit of a nightmare' – drives us out onto the western breakwater, a strong, tidily constructed white causeway which curves away towards the horizon. I can't see the end of it.

James fills me in on the size and scale of what they call the Al Faw Grand Port project. It is being built on desert land, which means there has been no population to physically displace. But the whole area saw some of the fiercest fighting of the Iran–Iraq war and subsequently the

Gulf war, so it had to be extensively, and expensively, de-mined before any work could begin. They're still finding bodies which have to be reported to the police and their DNA taken. The sea bed will also have to be cleared of mines. Then there was the issue of the fishermen in the nearby town of Al Faw. The digging and clearing and building of the breakwater directly affected their livelihood. They've now been given work on the project. In fact, James is very keen to let me know that 70 per cent of the workforce are local Iraqis.

I ask how long it will be before the first ships will be able to use the port. The contract, he tells me, is for five years with delays. 'And there's always delays.' He reckons at least seven years.

The plans are grandiose, involving railway connections across the desert and a new road running sixty or so miles into Iraq and accessed from the port through an underground tunnel.

I meet another Englishman. He's the head of contracts. If it all works out, he says, this huge project could transform Iraq. The 'if' is as large as the ambition, but as we drive back across the longest break-water in the world it looks pretty clear that they've invested too much time, money and national prestige to give up now.

The shuttle of trucks bringing in material goes on round the clock, raising a constant cloud of dust, and I'm quite glad when we're clear of the port works and passing through the modest town of Al Faw on our way south. The road crosses over a series of canals connecting the town with the sea. There are fishing boats of many colours tied up in these murky rubbish-filled creeks, sacrificed presumably to the Grand Port that will change their owners' lives for ever.

A mile or two further on, the road runs out. This is as far as we can go. I'd love to have dipped my feet in the waters of the Gulf, but there is no way of getting out there. The road simply merges with the

salt-encrusted wasteland. There is nothing momentous or significant to mark the end of Iraq. Just an attempt at a fence, attached to which are weather-bleached posters bearing pictures of young men who died in the fight to defend their country and their religion. At least that's my interpretation. Nobody really seems to know.

There is a neat, if bizarre, similarity to where we started our journey. The salt-pan stretching from here to the sea is almost dazzlingly white, as were the snows in the Turkish highlands, which feed the waters of Lake Hazar, which feed the Tigris, which feeds half of Iraq.

Someone points to the west, and shading my eyes against a strong wind I can pick out on the horizon the hazy shapes of tall buildings. The outlines of Kuwait. Saddam Hussein, thinking himself emperor of all the Middle East, sought to pick it off. Instead, he incurred the wrath of

America, so bringing about his own downfall and years of brutal conflict.

Frustratingly, the land here is so flat that I can't see the mouth of the Shatt al-Arab away to the east, and miss the satisfaction of seeing the Tigris and the Euphrates empty into the sea.

But give or take a few hundred yards, we've gone as far as we planned to go. And there were many times on this journey, mostly in the early mornings in strange hotels, when I wondered if we would ever get this far.

Back to Basra. Not much time for celebrating. We have a 5.30 start tomorrow and we're in an alcohol-free hotel in an alcohol-free city. But never underestimate the ingenuity of a good tour guide. James appears at the buffet with his familiar and much-appreciated coffee flask. Except that tonight the coffee tastes awfully like red wine.

DAY 18
اليوم الثامن عشر
Thursday 31ˢᵗ March

THE ALARM SOUNDS. IT'S 5.01. IT'S EARLY BUT WE'RE being cautious. We have to catch the flight to Istanbul or we won't get home today, and though we may see ourselves as adventurers and explorers on days when we're on top of a ziggurat or following flaming torches up a mountainside, today we just want to return to our families.

The city is dark and Basra's highways are almost deserted. On the eastern horizon I see the first light of dawn. Except that when I look more closely, it isn't dawn at all. The light in the eastern sky is from the oilfields. The plumes from scores of burn-off towers are mimicking the rising sun.

The thirst for oil is what created Iraq almost a hundred years ago, but there are many we talked to who see it as more of a curse than a blessing. The vast revenues from oil brought with them British interference in the region in the 1920s and the drawing of the borders of a new nation that largely ignored the different cultures of the people they contained. They helped fire Saddam's disastrous dreams and the equally disastrous consequences that followed his removal. The oil riches have been unable to stem the sectarian conflicts which seem endemic to the country. Because the oil money rolls in, there has been little incentive to tap the skills and talents of the Iraqi people to create other sources of national wealth.

For Iraq, the desert is the gift that keeps on giving. But sadly, after travelling through the length and breadth of the country, I feel that

somewhere blessed with such incredibly valuable resources should look better and feel better than it does.

We head out of town beneath a gantry sign with two diverging arrows. One reads '*Airport*', the other '*Iranian Border*'.

As we turn away to the airport I look out of the window for one last glance at the false dawn.

It seems like a fitting image with which to remember Iraq.

POSTSCRIPT

I'VE BEEN BACK HOME FOR A WHILE NOW, AND, THINKING back through my memories of my time in Iraq, I realise how fortunate I was to have such access to the country. I'm also aware that some of my memories are critical ones. I always try to be positive about travel and its benefits, but there's no getting away from the fact that Iraq arouses mixed feelings. It's a country that has so much to offer, but it's also one where the conflicts of the last decades have drained the energies of the people. There is a palpable feeling of waste, of potential dissipated by war and suffering. That doesn't mean, though, that we in the West should turn our backs, especially as we must bear responsibility for our part in those conflicts.

My own visit has ensured that the country remains vividly in my mind. Once a door has been opened and you have been made welcome – however tentatively – then a connection has been made, in the same way that a neighbour you meet in the street becomes that much closer if you've been inside their house.

Like North Korea, which I visited four years ago, Iraq has done time as an international pariah. In North Korea the problem is autocratic rule centred around one family. In Iraq things are quite the opposite. It's a fragmented country in which unity has to jump through a lot of hoops. The Kurds in the north do their own thing, as do the Iranian-backed militias in the south, whilst somewhere in the middle a central authority struggles to run the country, continually fending off allegations of partisanship and corruption.

In foreign relations Iraq seems to be pulled in two directions. Towards Turkey in the north and west, especially in Kurdistan, and towards Iran in the south, with its overt backing of the Shia clerics and their followers.

So far as Iraqi society is concerned, one thing that saddened me during my time in the country was the virtual invisibility of women in public life. Despite almost a third of those elected to the parliament in Baghdad in 2021 being women, there is no sense of them having an equal share in the country. Illiteracy in girls is double that of boys and the latest UN figures show only 14 per cent of Iraqi women in employment as opposed to 73 per cent of men.

There are signs of hope. The economy is booming. Iraq's oil revenues are higher than at any time in the last fifty years. In March 2022, oil and natural gas exports earned the country a record $11.7 billion. But as oil revenues boom, water resources continue to shrink. Three years of drought have reduced them by 50 per cent.

In the barren fields of Hashim's farm in Duluiyah I saw the reality of the water shortage: hard baked earth and a lost harvest. With the war in Ukraine drastically reducing global grain supplies there could hardly be a worse time for crops to fail.

That Iraq has these problems should not mean that we turn away: not just because they need all the friends they can get, but because we need all the friends we can get.

I'm glad I went to Iraq and I would go back, for the one reason that I met many good people there, and I should like to see them again.

Michael Palin
June 2022

CHRONOLOGY

ANCIENT IRAQ

c.10,000 BCE Beginnings of agriculture in the Middle East

c.5000–1750 Sumerian civilisation in the Euphrates–Tigris region

c.3800 Foundation of the city of Ur

c.3500 Invention of the wheel

c.3400 First writing system (cuneiform) developed
in Mesopotamia

c.2100 Ziggurat built in Ur

c.1894–1595 First Babylonian empire

c.900 Rise of the Assyrian empire in northern Mesopotamia

605–562 Nebuchadnezzar II rules in Babylon

539 Babylon conquered by Cyrus of Persia

c.312–63 Seleucid empire arises in Mesopotamia after division
of Macedonian empire created by Alexander the Great

115–117 CE Rome occupies Mesopotamia

224 Foundation of the Sasanian empire, which at its height
controls present-day Iran and Iraq

FROM the RISE of ISLAM to the BRITISH MANDATE

633 CE First Muslim invasion of Mesopotamia

680 The Battle of Karbala, at which two of Muhammad's grandsons perish

762 Baghdad founded as the capital of the Abassid caliphate. It becomes a centre of culture and science

1258 Baghdad is destroyed by the Mongols

1401 The Turco-Mongol warlord Timur (Tamerlane) invades Baghdad and kills many of its citizens

1534 The region now called Iraq becomes part of the Ottoman empire

1917 Britain seizes Baghdad during the First World War

1920 The three Ottoman administrative districts (vilayets) of Mosul, Baghdad and Basra are brought together, under British rule, as Iraq

1921 Britain appoints Faisal as King of Iraq

1932 Britain grants Iraq independence

MODERN IRAQ

1958 Iraqi monarchy overthrown in a left-wing military coup led by Abd al-Karim Qasim

1968 Coup led by Arab nationalist Ba'ath party puts Ahmad Hasan al-Bakr in power

1979 Saddam Hussein takes over from President al-Bakr

1980–88 Iran–Iraq war results in stalemate and 250,000 dead on either side

1990 Iraq invades Kuwait. US-led military campaign forces Iraq to withdraw in February 1991

1991 Rebellion against Saddam Hussein by southern Shia and northern Kurdish populations defeated

2003 US-led invasion topples Saddam Hussein's government, leading to his capture in December and execution in 2006

2011 Last US troops leave Iraq. Unity government divided and sectarian violence on the rise

2014 Islamic State (Daesh) seizes Mosul

2017 Government forces drive Islamic State out of most areas

2020 US drone strike kills Iranian General Qassim Soleimani and Iraqi militia leader Abu Mahdi al-Mohandes at Baghdad airport

A CIP catalogue record for this book is
available from the British Library

ISBN 978-1-529-15311-8

Publisher: Nigel Wilcockson

Assistant Editor: Elena Roberts

Designer: Tim Barnes,
www.herechickychicky.com

Map: Darren Bennett,
www.dkbcreative.com

Illustrations:
iStock.com/azat1976 (pp. iv, 34, 86, 168);
iStock.com/MartaJonina (pp. 8, 46, 94, 138);
iStock.com/Roman_Volkov (pp. 14, 56, 112,
152); iStock.com/NatBasil (pp. 22, 66, 124,
160); iStock.com/Sergio-Lucci (pp. 30, 74,
132, 164)

Printed and bound in Italy
by L.E.G.O. S.p.A.

The authorised representative in the EEA is
Penguin Random House Ireland,
Morrison Chambers, 32 Nassau Street,
Dublin D02 YH68.

www.greenpenguin.co.uk

Penguin Random House
is committed to a sustainable future for
our business, our readers and our planet.
This book is made from Forest Stewardship
Council® certified paper.

1 3 5 7 9 10 8 6 4 2

Hutchinson Heinemann

20 Vauxhall Bridge Road
London SW1V 2SA

Hutchinson Heinemann is part of
the Penguin Random House group of
companies whose addresses can be found
at global.penguinrandomhouse.com

Penguin
Random House
UK

Into Iraq
Copyright © Michael Palin, 2022

Michael Palin has asserted his right
to be identified as the author of this
Work in accordance with the Copyright,
Designs and Patents Act 1988

Photographs are reproduced
by kind permission of:
Doug Dreger pp. 4, 12, 13, 18, 20, 32, 48,
53, 58, 64 (top), 79, 80, 88, 90, 92, 99, 100,
103, 109, 119, 120–21, 122, 128, 130;
Neil Ferguson pp. 5, 10, 41, 54, 62–63,
64 (bottom), 68, 76, 78, 91, 104, 108, 111, 117,
127, 137, 145; Getty Images pp. 141, 162–163;
Jaimie Gramston pp. 39, 51, 52, 103, 135, 143.
All other photographs: Michael Palin.

First published by Hutchinson Heinemann
in 2022

www.penguin.co.uk

MIX
Paper from
responsible sources
FSC® C016897